Functional Java:

A Guide to Lambdas and Functional Programming in Java 8

By Nick Maiorano

Functional Java:

A Guide to Lambdas and Functional Programming in Java 8
By Nick Maiorano

The team:

Editor:	Erik LeBel
Copy editor:	Nathalie Laroche
Technical reviewers:	Olivier Croisier
	Larry Presswood
	Steven Haines
Cover art:	Konrad Rosochacki

Publishing history

Kindle edition:	April 2014
Print edition:	June 2014

ISBN-10: 0-9937050-0-6

ISBN-13: 978-0-9937050-0-7

Table of Contents

Preface

With the release of Java 8, the language has undergone the most radical transformation in its history. It has altered itself from being an imperative, structured, object-oriented, generic, reflective, and concurrent programming language to one that offers all of the above plus a unique take on functional programming. While there are important syntactical and library changes in this update, the most important change will occur in the minds of Java developers as they use the new language constructs to solve every day programming problems. This is the functionalization of Java. There are, of course, other additions not related to functional programming, but from this book's point of view, discussing anything else would be like talking about the weather upon the birth of your child. The analogy is apropos since, after all, this is the birth of a brand new functional Java.

Oracle's long-awaited eighth version of Java will have a huge impact on the world of software. The Java set of technologies—including the language, JVM, standard libraries, standard/enterprise/mobile editions, as well as open source and commercial offerings—have collectively created a massive footprint in software. There are an estimated eight million Java developers in the world and innumerable Java applications ranging from mission critical to hardly critical at all. It's a resounding success by any measure but it's never been smooth sailing. Java continues to fight in the trenches with new ideas, trends, and technologies. Since it's a general-purpose language with a wide footprint spanning mobile, desktop, back-end, front-end, enterprise, and cloud, it battles on many fronts. Sometimes it wins (Java on the server-side), sometimes it loses (J2ME). Through it all, Java has achieved and maintained a top-tier status amongst programming languages in terms of adoption. Even today, with the world of software development more fragmented than ever, Java still maintains its elite status. And yet, there has never been a more important release for the future of Java.

> Java has undergone the most radical transformation in its history

Due to its massive user base, the Java syntax and standard libraries have adopted a brand of conservatism rivalled only by the Vatican. With the exception of Java 5 and the introduction of generics and enums, the syntax has hardly evolved over time. While some methods in the standard library have been deprecated, not a single one of these has been completely removed. Backward binary compatibility has been guaranteed for every release. While this is good for the acquired user base, it's bad for keeping up with emerging language paradigms. Brian Goetz, the Java language architect, declared that Java must evolve. Java 8 is a bold attempt at that.

This book is written *by* a Java software professional *for* Java software professionals. It's aimed particularly at developers coming from an object-oriented, imperative background with little or no prior exposure to functional programming. It may also be useful to those already using functional languages and who have an interest in understanding how Java realizes its functional self. JSR-335 (lambda support) is the main driver of Java 8. It culminates seven years of work and missed deadline (lambdas were initially planned for Java 7) and represents a quite technical feat in retrofitting a foreign paradigm onto a mature language. However, this comes with its own set of compromises. After all, any change needs to co-exist with a language that has its own culture and way of doing things. Anyone coming from a pure functional language may be disappointed and perceive Java to be a watered-down functional language. I consider this to be an unfair criticism. Java is still an object-oriented language at its core. The goal was never to erase that dominant trait but rather to compliment it and offer new tools to better solve new problems. The longer-term strategy is to gradually nudge Java developers into a more functional way of doing things and this will take several releases. After all, Rome wasn't built in a day and Java won't be changed in one either. In the end, Java will implement its own distinctive functional blend.

Unlike previous updates, mastering this one will take some time because it's not just about syntax; it's a brand new programming paradigm. You will have to rewire parts of your programming brain to solve problems in a functional way. It will impact everything, starting from your high-level design choices to your low-level algorithms. There is nothing harder in computer programming, or in life, than to change your daily habits.

A number of new functional languages have gained popularity in recent years and all other major programming languages have incorporated functional elements. For the Java developer, there's nowhere left to hide. You will be exposed to functional concepts whether you are ready or not. Of course, the fact that you're reading this book demonstrates your interest in contributing to this revolution.

I've constructed this book to help you learn the subject matter in three stages:

- Mastery of the new *syntax*
- Mastery of the new *libraries*
- Mastery of functional *concepts*

This is similar to learning a new language: first you learn the words (*syntax*), then you learn how to structure sentences (*libraries*), finally you learn how to think in that language (*concepts*). You don't master the French language by thinking in English and translating each word. You master it by immersing yourself in the French culture until you become... French! In the same way, you will not master the functional side of Java by thinking imperatively then translating to functional constructs. You think functionally until you become... functional! This will require patience. For some, learning about lambdas and functional programming will remind you of your college days when you struggled with new programming concepts. I was reminded of my software infancy when struggling with pointer types in the Pascal programming language. While it did not take great intellect to grasp the concept, it took much more practice to reason about them with mental agility. Lambdas have proven to be similar in their deceiving simplicity.

The goal of this book is to answer these grand questions:

- What is functional programming?
- How has Java adopted functional programming?
- How can functional programming be used in everyday Java?

Writing this book has been a rewarding experience. I hope reading it will be the same for you.

Conventions

Code examples are shown in tables with a shaded background. For the sake of brevity, most code examples are not shown in their entirety. This means that they may not compile as is but would require the usual glue to get them to execute (including import statements, main methods, etc.). Full code examples can be obtained at *http://thoughtflow.ca/en/functionaljava/codeexamples.*

When code is discussed outside of the table, any specific reference to a method name, variable, operand, or any other part of the Java syntax or library is displayed in italics. Within code samples, the bold font is used to draw attention to specific portions of the code while strike through is used to depict deleted or incorrect code.

Comments and Questions

Please address all comments and questions to *info@thoughtflow.ca.*

Acknowledgments

I would like to thank my exceptional team who helped make this book a reality: to Olivier, Larry, and Steven for helping me stand on solid ground, to Nathalie for her enthusiasm and professionalism in helping me get the right phrasing, and finally to Erik for being the problem solver, motivator, and friend.

I'd also like to thank my wife and son, who for the last 18 months have accepted and made the necessary sacrifices for me to write this book.

This book is dedicated to the little demons that live inside our heads and tell us not to do things. Whether it's mastering Java 8 or writing a book about mastering Java 8, it's best we acknowledge their existence and proceed anyway.

Part I
The juncture of functional programming & Java

Chapter 1: Introduction

The year was 1996. End-of-millennium anxieties were beginning to set in the collective consciousness. Nostradamus and Y2K COBOL programmers were predicting doomsday scenarios. Dolly the sheep was the first mammal to be cloned while grunge music, which by that time had done a good deal of self-cloning, was ceding its place to boy bands. Stock markets around the world were soaring to new heights while the tech bubble was still in its infancy. At the time, only 45 million people used the Internet (about 0.75% of the world's population). *Surfing* was now becoming a land-based activity that one would typically do using a Netscape browser, a Windows 95 operating system, and a 200 MHz Pentium Pro machine. Things were hard to find before Google came along but in retrospect, there wasn't that much to find. The Gang of Four had just released their *Design Patterns* book, forever changing our software vocabulary, while the Three Amigos[1] were creating their unified modeling language (UML), forever changing our software diagrams. There was also the release of an obscure new language named Java by Sun Microsystems.

There wasn't much of a struggling period for Java as it quickly drew the attention of software managers,

> **The virtual machine was the main reason Java would flourish as a top-tier language**

architects, and developers. Adoption was swift. By building upon a familiar C++ syntax and removing features deemed problematic, Java was conceived as a better C++, the dominant language of the time. Of course, Java had the luxury; it didn't have an established user base to serve and could start on a clean slate. So operator overloading, pointer arithmetic, and multiple inheritance were out while code clarity, strong typing, and interfaces were in. It was designed around object-orientation, which in 1996 was the price of admission for a programming language. Object-orientation would become part of the Java DNA and still remains an important tool in taming code complexity, size, and structure.

Java was also conceived to run on top of a virtual machine. This enabled the underlying hardware to be abstracted away. With its write-once-run-anywhere mantra, integers would be 32-bit creatures on big iron Solaris UNIX machines as well as Windows-based

---

[1] Grady Booch, Ivar Jacobson and James Rumbaugh

desktops. As archaic as this concern may seem today, program portability was a big problem that had plagued previous generation C++ applications. The virtual machine also enabled something of much greater importance: automated garbage collection. This took developers out of the business of memory lifecycle management and into higher-level concerns. While some memory leaks would continue to exist in Java applications, the beast would be tamed. Despite this, garbage collection was not an easy sell and there would be many critics doubting the efficiency of automated garbage collection. By the turn of the century, massive improvements in garbage collection strategies would silence the sceptics and convince most that Java was for real and could be used even in the most demanding conditions.

The virtual machine would also have unforeseen consequences. First, it enabled libraries to flourish. One of Java's greatest strength would become its sheer volume of libraries in the standard, open source, and commercial spaces. Libraries could be greatly simplified because there was no need to define object disposition in the API. No need for smart-pointers and no possibility of forgetting dispose of memory. The virtual machine would take care of it all. While the concept of a virtual machine was not new, it would create a feedback loop whereby developers would flock to Java because libraries were there and libraries would flock to Java because the developers were there.

The second unforeseen consequence would be that it would allow foreign languages to leverage the virtual machine. Since the virtual machine would have its own native byte code language, a foreign language could compile to byte code and run on the virtual machine. A new generation of languages, including Scala, Clojure, and Groovy, could innovate within the safe confines of the virtual machine eco-system. This would create a separate asset for the Java community that could evolve independently of the Java language but still maintain the relevance of Java—a way of hedging the bets on future technologies. Ultimately, the virtual machine, with its garbage collection, hardware abstraction, and language platform, would be the catalyst in enabling Java to flourish as a top-tier language in the following decades.

A new generation of programming languages would gain mindshare in the second half of the 2000s. They were all based on the functional programming paradigm.

The history of functional programming

Functional programming, like most things in computer science, is nothing new. It has a long history in academia that traces its roots to lambda calculus, a branch of mathematics created by renowned mathematician Alonzo Church. First formulated in 1936, lambda calculus found multiple fields of application but first gained prominence in computational theory and later in computer science, giving birth to the LISP programming language in 1958. LISP, one of the world's oldest programming language, would become the world's first functional language. It has had a long evolution spawning multiple dialects including Common Lisp, Scheme, ISLISP, and Clojure, all of which are still in use today. Not all functional languages can trace their ancestry from LISP but they were still very much influenced by it as well as lambda calculus. The common thread is the culture of academia that permeates functional languages. These are, after all, languages used to express advanced mathematical concepts.

The functional community expends considerable energy debating the functional purity of their pet language. Such is the case that functional languages come in two flavors: pure and impure. This is in reference to how strictly the language adheres to functional principles. Haskell, named after mathematician Haskell Curry, is the most prominent and pure functional language. The impure kind is a broader one and its leaders include Scala, Erlang, OCaml, Scheme, ML, and Clojure. Even within the impure category, it's a sliding scale from languages that mix multiple programming paradigms to others that only support functional programming albeit in a less than pure way. Scala embraces both object-oriented and functional paradigms whereas Clojure is not pure but only supports functional programming. There is a whiff of religion to this business of discussing purity of functional languages. This is part and parcel of the functional community.

Not coincidentally, the number of pure languages is much smaller than the number of impure ones. This is because functional programming can be challenging and demanding. Making languages less functional and relaxing their constraints make them more accessible to the masses and more usable to those who ship software.

The Java community has been tormented for years debating whether or not functional concepts should be added. Early in Java's history, the language architects considered adding functional concepts but decided against it because it was deemed too difficult for the average programmer. By 2007, functional languages were gaining popularity and the Java community was forced to reconsider its position. In response, a pre-JSR project named "the BGGA project" (consisting of Gilad Bracha, Neal Gafter, James Gosling, and Peter von der Ahé) was initiated to investigate the idea of functionalizing Java. This led to a prototype named CICE that allowed the Java community to experiment with the idea. Finally JSR-335 was filed in November of 2009. After years of development, missed releases, deadlines pushed back, and growing developer impatience, Java 8 was released in March of 2014. In all, it took seven years to functionalize Java. This was amid a community torn between adapting to changes and preserving the

> It took seven years to functionalize Java

integrity of a successful language. Why was there so much controversy and why did it take so much time? To answer these questions, we need to explore what functional programming is and why we need it.

What is functional programming?

Functional programming predates Java by almost 40 years but its virtues have only recently been fully appreciated by the mainstream. The functional paradigm consists of a set of principles that include:

- The treatment of functions as first-class citizens of the language
- The avoidance of residual state and the emphasis on immutability
- The avoidance of side effects

It's no accident that these principles describe mathematical functions precisely. Generally in mathematics and particularly in calculus, functions represent the chief abstraction of the language. Everything is expressed in terms of a function. It's not the first-class citizen of the language; it's the *only* class citizen of the language. Second, mathematical functions have no concept of residual state. That is, functions are computed and values are returned. There is no conversational history between the caller and the function. This is closely tied to the third principle of avoiding side effects: a function will yield the same result for the same parameter. No prior computation or timing can affect the outcome. Notice that I used the words "avoidance" and "emphasis" rather than stronger words such as "prohibition" and "enforcement". Functional languages vary in their commitment to these ideologies.

These concepts are already well known and understood in Java and in computer science at large. For example, Java supports the *final* variable declaration (immutability) and *static* methods (avoidance of class state). Java does not impede a programmer from expressing behavior through class methods (functions as first-class constructs) and avoiding side effects. There is nothing particularly radical about these ideas and the guiding set of principles can be encapsulated by stating that there is no state in functional programming—except for your state of mind. Functional programming is first and foremost about how you see and solve problems rather than any particular syntax in the language. What is important to the evolution of software languages is the widespread recognition that these

There is no state in functional programming—except for your state of mind

principles are particularly useful in solving modern concurrency problems in software engineering.

Moore's law, RIP

In 1965, Gordon Moore famously wrote about the doubling of transistors on integrated circuits, which doubled performance every two years and gave birth to "Moore's law". He based this on his own observations dating back to 1958 and predicted that the trend would last another ten years. In reality, he was wrong; the trend would continue for another 40 years! In fact, the number of transistors has kept on doubling but clock speeds have stagnated since about 2000 (see figure 1) and flat-lined in 2005. To compensate, chip manufacturers have responded with multi-core architectures. This had a profound impact in the world of software engineering and particularly in server-side computing. For years, software engineers could always rely on vertical scaling to solve performance bottlenecks. If the application could not scale to meet demand, the easy way out was to throw money at the problem and get a bigger machine with more CPU power—the very definition of vertical scaling. This was often easier and cheaper than re-engineering the application. With the rise of multi-core CPU architectures, the proverbial *free lunch* was over. Software could no longer automatically benefit from newer multi-core machines. Instead, software needed to be re-engineered.

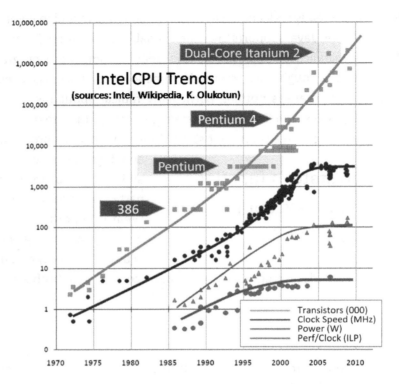

Figure 1: CPU trends (From Herb Sutter, The Free Lunch is Over)

The typical way to increase throughput from a server-side application has been to multi-thread the application. From the start, Java has had built-in thread constructs that make it easy to spawn new threads. The difficult part has been guaranteeing the correctness, performance, and scalability of complex, multi-threaded programs.

Software organizations have typically given the task of implementing multi-threaded programs to senior developers. Care has been given to ensure that shared mutable state is controlled with locks and carry-and-swap (CAS) atomics. These locks must then be manually released. Forgetting to release a lock or locking in an inefficient way could be catastrophic for an application. Even in the most capable hands, this programming model has been flawed because it is impossible to guarantee the correctness of a multi-threaded program through static analysis. Relying on runtime analysis fares no better because bugs can go undetected in quality assurance testing and only manifest themselves in a production environment. Trying to reproduce errors and ensuring they are fixed has always been something of a black art.

Furthermore, traditional multi-threaded programs don't take full advantage of the CPU's multi-core architecture. This is because there is no core awareness at the application level. Instead, their abstraction of the hardware is one of threads time-sharing a CPU. This is particularly inefficient for CPU-intensive programs.

If we adhere to functional programming's set of principles, we can design applications that are better suited for multi-core CPUs. By avoiding states and adhering to immutability, we can eliminate shared locks and the class of bugs they produce. If we avoid side effects, we can reorder execution and distribute workload across multiple cores. If we express our code through a series of functions, we can delegate more of the low-level drudgery to the language and focus on higher-level concerns. By giving up some of the control, the language can then offer better efficiencies. This is similar to the deal we made with garbage collection: let the garbage collector handle memory management and it will give us better overall performance

Functional-style parallelism is an abstraction leak but it is the best way to extract more performance from saturated CPUs

through wholesale efficiencies. Functional programming is not a panacea but it does offer a new set of tools to solve old problems.

We cannot complete this section without mentioning that there is a blemish on the face of functional-style parallelism. Like it or not, the industry has taken us to the point where multi-core technology is omni-present. In a way, functional programming represents an abstraction leak that alters the view of the underlying hardware. With conventional multi-threaded programs, the CPU is a black box. Java programs interact with the JVM, which, in turn, creates threads in the operating system. The operating system then manages all CPU thread scheduling and shields every other layer from these details. Thus a multi-threaded application works without knowing the details of the CPU architecture. The Java virtual machine is all about abstracting the hardware and making integers look the same regardless of addressing capabilities. Functional programming proposes a model, which exposes the inner details of the CPU architecture and allows the cores to be manipulated from several layers up. This creates an abstraction leak because it doesn't protect programs from changes to the underlying hardware. What would happen if multi-core CPUs would be superseded by new single-core technology? A generation of applications built specifically for multi-core CPUs would no longer be fully compatible with new hardware improvements. Traditional multi-threaded programs do a better job at abstracting the hardware. Like in any interface design, an interface client should not know how the API gets the job done—just that it will get done. Functional-style parallelism breaks the contract and this may be a monumental abstraction leak. Nevertheless, it's a deal the industry accepted because it squeezes more performance out of saturated CPUs.

Conciseness—the dark side of functional programming

We've only just scratched the surface of functional programming but we are beginning to paint a more descriptive image. Functional programming has its own distinctive soul, which, naturally, comes from the world of mathematics. Lambda calculus is itself concise, driven by symbols; functional languages reflect this both in syntax and expressions. This results in code that is typically terse and dense. Functional programmers take great pride in demonstrating how much they can do with as little code as possible, but this goes even further. Functional languages have a toolbox of constructs that allow you to code at a higher level of abstraction. This is somewhat like programming on top of a framework that lets you re-arrange blocks in new and powerful ways. You re-arrange and customize these blocks with small bits of code in the same way Linux allows you to chain commands together. When we chain Linux commands such as *netstat —an | grep LISTENING | grep 80* we are actually applying functional concepts to determine, in this case, whether or not an HTTP server is ready.

The dark side of conciseness is code density and readability. It can be more difficult to grasp the essence of a line of functional code from a quick glance—especially from someone coming from the imperative world. This is because functional expressions do more with less code. Comprehension can be increased with a little practice but since there is more going on per square inch of screen, it usually takes a little more reasoning to understand the essence of a line of functional code. This is somewhat paradoxical: imperative code tends to breathe more and be easier to understand at the atomic level but is actually more difficult to grasp when looking at the entirety of an algorithm. Functional code is the opposite. It breathes less, is more dense, but communicates intent better. It is easier to understand once we zoom out.

Why has it taken so long to functionalize Java?

Now that we've highlighted some of the characteristics of functional programming, we can begin to explore the task of functionalizing Java. Why has it taken so long and why so much controversy? Based on this brief introduction into functional programming, it becomes apparent that you can't just bring these ideas into Java without considering the consequences. Java is a successful language and its stakeholders have been rightfully concerned about the possibility of destroying its essence. Can multiple programming paradigms really co-exist in one language? Java already has multiple personalities, each contributing to making it unique. It is an imperative, structured, object-oriented, generic, reflective, and concurrent programming language. Adding a seventh personality does not necessarily convolute it but it does have a huge impact. The Scala programming language has successfully blended many of these same elements to form a coherent whole. However, it had the luxury of starting from scratch. Java, on the other hand, has an established user base and a conservative approach to things. It's no wonder that the lambda project was years in the making.

To fully appreciate the challenges in incorporating functional programming, let's compare the worldviews of Java and functional programming based on the following twelve points.

1. Organization styles

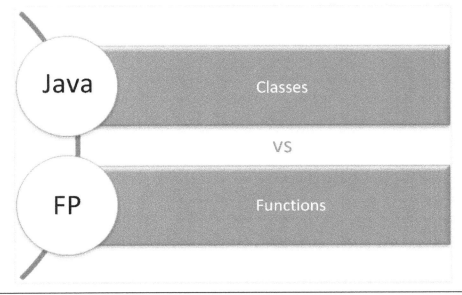

Objected-oriented programming and functional programming start from very different points in that they organize code differently. In object-orientation, class is king. Everything is organized within the context of a class. On the other hand, functional programming's currency is functions. In fact, in purely functional languages, there is no alternative but to write code within the context of a function. While functional purity varies among different languages, one constant remains: functional languages put great emphasis on the function. So there is an important chasm between the organization styles of the two.

2. Building blocks

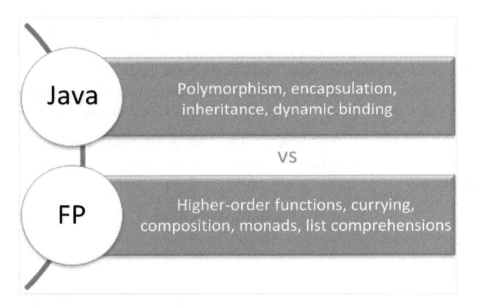

Once we move past the code organization, we use the available building blocks to start writing code. Here again, the two paradigms have very different approaches. Objected-orientation is a paradigm that focuses on code structure in its pursuit to be modular. This is primordial in reducing complexity and increasing maintainability of large systems. The tools at our disposal are polymorphism, encapsulation, inheritance, and dynamic binding; each contributes to structuring code by putting state with methods, reducing code size, enabling reuse, and making things maintainable. Functional programming's main concern is behavior. Higher-order functions (functions that take other functions as parameters and/or return functions), currying (partial application of a function's parameter to get another function that takes one less argument), composition (functions composed of other functions), monads (composition of functions that have side effects), and list comprehensions (applying functions to lists) are all examples of behavior-centric building blocks. Although incomplete, this glimpse into functional programming shows us that its concerns are more focused on behavior than structure. This is an important distinction.

3. Algorithmic styles

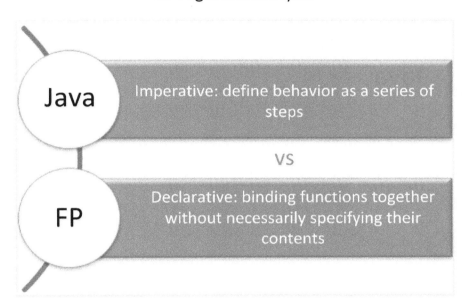

Java relies on object-orientation to provide structure, but within this structure is imperative programming. Imperative programming is a fundamental way of doing things; it is used in many computer languages and is deeply embedded in the way we solve problems. It defines behavior as a series of sequential steps. In reality, there are other ways of doing things. The functional model proposes a declarative approach whereby programmers bind functions together without necessarily specifying their steps. This is inherently a higher-level of abstraction because lower-level implementation concerns are relinquished. This enables economies of scale to happen and can lead to code optimization driven by the language. Furthermore, some functional languages can automatically change execution order for the sake of optimization. For the imperative problem solver, this can be a challenge and a commitment must be made to accept the fact that some things will be easier while others will be harder. It's a trade-off.

Functional programming predisposes developers into thinking about code in terms of re-arrangeable blocks. This results in code that can be rearranged in new and unanticipated ways and creates a system whose whole is greater than the sum of its parts.

4. State management

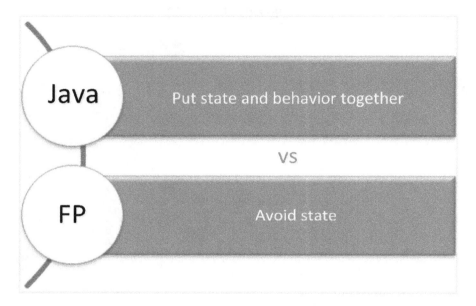

Putting state and behavior together, the idea behind encapsulation is one of the main tenets of object-oriented programming. During its ascension to mainstream consciousness in the 1990s, object-oriented programming promised to fix some of the shortcomings of procedural programming, namely state management. Procedural programming did not adequately delineate state and code that used it. This would result in a free-for-all access scenario whereby there were no mechanisms in place to control access to state. This void crippled large systems and made it more difficult to manage larger application footprints. Fortunately, systems were a lot smaller by today's standards. Object-oriented languages, such as Java, had an answer for this and were designed with access controls to methods and attributes (e.g., public, protected, private, and default). Consequently, data was encapsulated by the code using it, which enabled large application code bases to flourish. Unfortunately, it did not address the other problem with state management: how to properly manage access to states in a concurrent environment.

Functional programming comes from a mathematical world where there is no state other than the transitional state. Where object-oriented is about creating objects, interacting with them, and maintaining conversational state, functional programming is about calling functions, returning a value, and having no further conversational state. While functional programming does use states, it is not of the conversational or residual kind. For example, the stack frame via recursion or argument passing is a common technique for maintaining some form of short-lived state.

5. Mutability

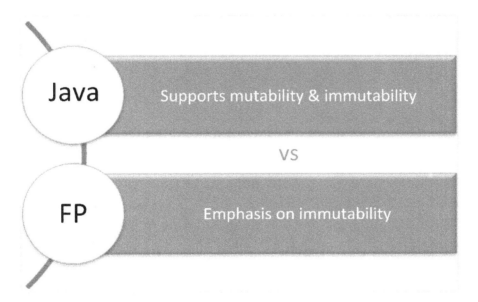

Java does not take a philosophical stand in regards to mutability of states. It supports mutability by default and allows object references to be immutable with the *final* keyword. Beyond that, it remains neutral. Functional programming does take a stand and champions the virtues of immutability. In functional languages, this varies from an outright ban on changing the state once a variable has been assigned to a more watered down version where mutability is allowed but the programmer is encouraged to favor immutability. As is often stated in functional literature, it is true that it is much easier to reason about a program if it embraces immutability.

6. Functional purity

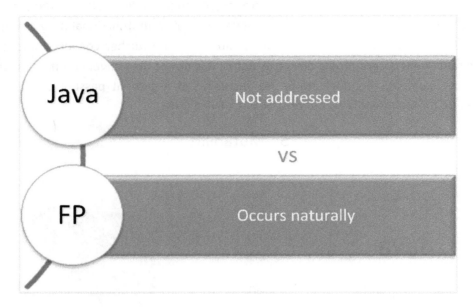

Functional purity, or the notion of functions having no side effects, is the end result we get when we apply functional principles to our software design. When a function can be called repeatedly with the same parameters and yield the same result, it is said to be a pure function. It is achieved if we avoid states and strive for immutability. The function cannot maintain conversation states that could affect the outcome with multiple calls. Functional purity helps reduce complexity because we can factor out state change when ensuring that a function behaves correctly. It is also a fundamental principle of functional-style parallelism. Java and object-orientation have no real answer for functional purity.

7. Design Patterns

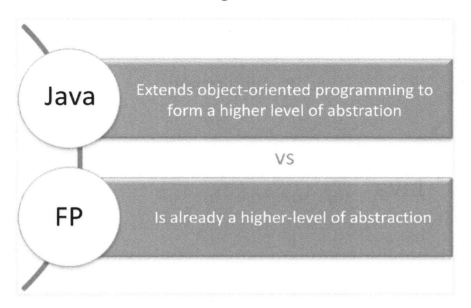

Java — Extends object-oriented programming to form a higher level of abstration

VS

FP — Is already a higher-level of abstraction

Object-oriented programming and Design Patterns go hand in hand. It can be said that Design Patterns complete object-orientation. This is because object-orientation is a lower level of abstraction and Design Patterns provide the filler that elevates software design to solve modern problems. Functional programming starts at a higher level of abstraction and doesn't require what some might call a crutch that Design Patterns is to object-orientation. In fact, many of the patterns found in the Gang of Four's *Design Patterns* book are no longer needed in the functional world because they are so basic. Design Patterns are simply recipes to solve common problems. They tell us how to bake a cake. Functional languages come with the cake already baked! If a language has no construct or idiom for a for-loop, and for-loops are non-obvious and require a fair amount of code, then it makes sense to invent a recipe for them. If Design Patterns are for-loops, and a given language allows you to express them with one line of code, you no longer need a design pattern.

Some academic research suggests that 16 out of the 23 Gang of Four patterns can be eliminated outright in functional programming. I would add that any pattern whose usefulness is limited to returning an object containing behavior (hello factory patterns) is obsolete in functional programming. After all, this is the lambda's very reason for existing. The remaining seven patterns—Visitor, Composite, Singleton, Prototype, Adapter, Decorator, and Memento—may still be needed but are much simpler in functional patterns. Research is continuing in the field of functional patterns and these will augment functional programming's level of abstraction even further. There is no authoritative book that is equivalent to *Design Patterns* in the functional world to set the standard. Perhaps, there is no pressing need for one either.

8. Concurrency

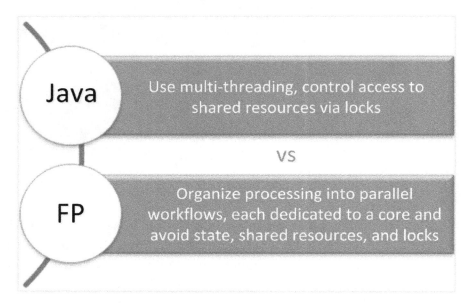

Since its inception, Java's answer to concurrency has been multi-threading. Threads have always been native to Java, not requiring the program to directly interact with the operating system to create them, and this has made it easy to use threads in Java. The difficultly has been in designing *correct* state management that works in highly concurrent environments. Over time, Java has greatly improved its offering with better abstractions in the locking libraries but the problem has persisted: the threading model is non-deterministic. Therefore, testing for program correctness is difficult and proving it is impossible. There is an infinite amount of execution paths to test. Safely and efficiently sharing state with concurrent threads is difficult to get right even for the most experienced developers. Deadlocks are a constant hazard.

With the advent of multi-core CPUs, Java's fork-join framework has stepped in to provide core awareness but the Java community has not changed its thinking to take advantage of it. In contrast, functional programming is a natural fit for multi-core CPUs because it avoids state and shared resources. This enables parallel workflows where work is segregated by cores. Functional programming is a paradigm that fits the times.

9. Recursion

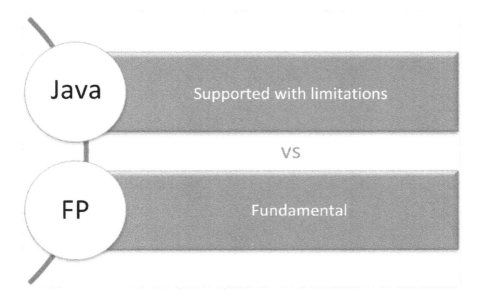

Recursion is a fundamental abstraction in functional programming. A language is said to be functional if it provides industrial strength for recursion. It must provide tail-call optimization, which allows a function to support deep recursion. In recursion, a stack frame is consumed in every iteration. This allows the state of local variables to be saved until the stack is unwound. However, if the last statement is a call to itself or any other function, there is no need to store the state because it will no longer be required after the stack unwinds (since it is the last statement). Tail-call optimized languages recognize this and avoid consuming another stack frame. This enables industrial strength recursion.

Java does not yet support tail-call optimization and therefore can lead to stack overflows. Depending on how much state is preserved on the stack, it doesn't take much to *blow the stack*. Based on this metric alone, Java 8 would not be a true functional language. Some lobbying has occurred in the past few years to make Java tail-call optimized, but since there hasn't been public outcry nor is it a trivial task, there are no planned changes. Java's new functional side may change the outlook. As a result, recursion must be used with caution or avoided and replaced with other techniques.

10.Code style

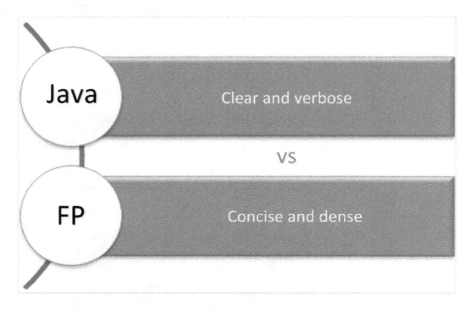

Java has had a bad rap for being too verbose. Part of this comes from its starting point. In the early days, Java was touted as being a better C++ doing away with many of the constructs that made life difficult for developers. In particular, a construct like operator overloading was one such example of abuse. It allowed developers to give new semantics to common constructs such as the + operator and to create a domain-specific language. Unless well thought out, this type of overloading often led to subtle side effects for unsuspecting developers using these objects despite the fact that they led to very concise code. The Java creators instead sought the path to clarity and traded conciseness for clarity and verbosity. This trade-off was widely accepted at the time.

The pendulum has now swung back as functional languages tout the virtues of conciseness. Functional languages also encourage a style of chaining function calls together resulting in code that is not only concise but also dense.

Java faces more headwind if it aims to become less verbose: object-orientation is an inherently verbose conversational paradigm. You create an object, you set its state, you mutate its state, and you get its state. This back and forth creates a larger code footprint than its functional equivalent. Many JDK libraries are written this way. Generics, which are used heavily in Java-style functional programming, also produce large code footprints, as does the use of primitives.

11.Influences

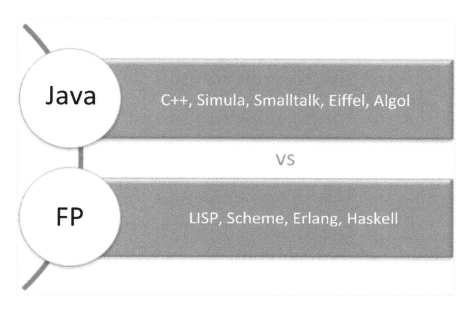

Java is the great-grandchild of many ancestral languages. Its bloodline consists of popular languages such as C++, with which it shares a similar syntax, as well as Smalltalk and Eiffel, with which it shares its object-oriented DNA. Functional programming languages have a very different lineage including LISP and other dialects as well as the early functional languages Haskell, Scheme, and Erlang. This is a stark reminder that Java and functional programming come from very different backgrounds.

12.Community

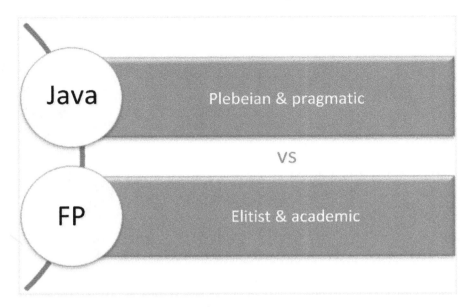

Every language comes with its own distinct community. It is important to understand that culture and to respect it whenever we learn a new language. The Java community comes from a position of ubiquity. It is a more plebeian and pragmatic community concerned with shipping software. The functional programming community is by and large more elitist and academic. This is congruent with its mathematical origins. The community can be overly concerned with software as an end rather than viewing software as a means to an end. Perhaps this is a simplified view but I think it helps in setting the tone for things to come. Expect the Java community to be more pragmatic about its adoption of functional programming.

These points will be a recurring theme throughout the book. We will also specifically address several of these points in greater detail.

Dysfunctional Java?

With clashing worldviews, have efforts to make Java functional rendered it *dysfunctional*? The reality is that it has not. Java's core traits have remained intact. Functional elements have been incorporated pragmatically into the language. As a developer, you take what you need and use the best tool for the job. You can use functional features when they make sense and stick to good old object-oriented code otherwise. Minimal changes have been made to the language syntax to accommodate functional programming; most of the functional flavor comes from the new libraries. In keeping with its longstanding conservative tradition, Java 8 is fully backward compatible. This way, you can opt in or out like you would with any other library. Java's functional adoption is not a matter of philosophical righteousness but rather of doing what's best for you. We don't need to judge Java based on how functionally pure it is but rather on its ability to solve certain problems in a functional way if required.

The language architects have hit the sweet spot in balancing legacy and functional in Java 8

As sensible as this sounds, discussions leading up to Java 8 have made some developers uneasy. Some were concerned about making Java 8 too functional and breaking a good thing, while others were concerned that it did not go far enough in comparison to other functional languages. Making both camps uncomfortable may be a sign that the language architects have hit the sweet spot in balancing legacy and functionality in Java 8.

Learning Java 8

There are varying degrees to which developers can adopt functional programming. Some may never use the lambdas and the functional libraries while others may just use lambdas but never embrace functional thinking. As previously mentioned, functional programming is much more than just syntax; it is an adherence to a set of principles and a state of mind. This is much harder to change.

Mastering Java 8 to its functional fullest would require a transition through four levels.

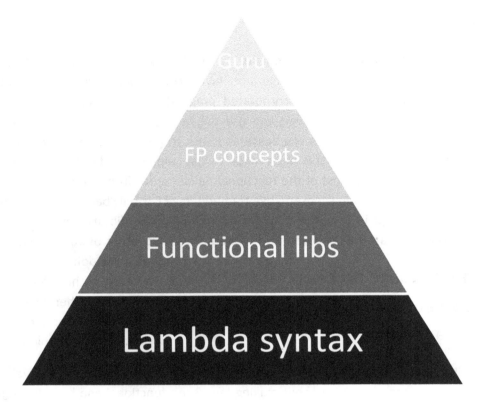

Figure 2: Path to Java 8 mastery

At the very basic level, you will learn about lambdas and the **lambda syntax**. This is the entry level to functional programming. Lambdas will become commonplace in Java 8 because they make things easier and will be part of many 3rd party APIs. But they are also deceivingly simple, so mastering them will require time and patience. It is important because the real magic only happens in the Java's **functional libraries** and having a solid grasp of lambdas is the price of admission. In the functional libraries, you can express functional code conceptually similar to other functional languages. Mastering these will require more than just learning the new APIs, but learning to think in functional terms as well. It is only after graduating from this stage that you will begin to apply **functional concepts** on your path to becoming a fully *functional* human being. This book is written with this approach in mind. We begin with the lambda syntax and the anatomy of the lambda.

Key points

- Java was conceived as a better C++ by improving upon its familiar syntax and offering a virtual machine that would abstract the underlying hardware and automate the lifecycle management of memory. It also offered a rich standard library.

- New languages were welcomed onto the virtual machine and since these were mostly functional, it helped push functional programming into the mainstream. New functional languages could use a mature platform that had become the Java virtual machine.

- The virtues of functional programming, with its emphasis on immutability, avoidance of state, and side effects, became increasingly apparent in the new millennium world of multi-core CPUs.

- Java 8 represents the most radical change in its history. Great care was taken to introduce functional programming over a seven-year period.

- Java's worldview can be incompatible with functional programming. In particular, its object-oriented, imperative nature sometimes clashes with functional concepts. Rather than change its DNA, functional programming has been blended into Java to complement its heritage. Developers will be able to tap into functional libraries if needed and functional programming will be treated as an add-on, not something that hijacks Java.

- Mastering functional programming in Java will be achieved in stages starting with lambdas, followed by functional libraries, and completed with the adherence to functional principles.

Part II
Anatomy of the lambda

Lambdas are to functional programming what words are to sentences: they convey thoughts and can be grouped together to create more complex thoughts. Just like you can't learn to write without first learning how to form a sentence, you won't learn functional programming without understanding lambdas. In part II, we will dissect the lambda as it applies to Java 8.

More specifically, you will learn:

- The lambda form
- Functional interfaces
- Method references
- Default and static methods
- Functional interface extension
- Lexical scoping rules

Be warned that if you are an experienced Java developer, you may actually be at a disadvantage. You may arrive with predispositions that will get in the way. As you read this chapter, you may be asking "what have they done to my Java?!"

The concept of lambdas is not terribly complicated but dealing with them with mental agility will take some time. As well, there are hidden traps lurking in the fine print. This section will discuss all of the syntactical changes made in Java 8 to support lambdas and functional programming. Without further ado, let's talk about the crown jewel of Java 8: the lambda.

Chapter 2: The lambda form

What's a lambda?

Named after the eleventh letter of the Greek alphabet, the lambda has its origins in calculus and computational theory. It was chosen by Alonzo Church as a notation to express his new form of calculus. Its application has since moved passed its mathematical roots and into other areas, including computer science. In functional programming, the term lambda has come to represent the idea of anonymous functions.

For many years leading up to the creation of Java 8, the term *closure* was used interchangeably with *lambda* in the Java community. The two are closely related but refer to slightly different concepts in functional programming terminology. In essence, lambdas are merely inline functions but in Java 8, lambdas are also closures because they enclose (inherit) the entire state of the class and method in which they are defined. By state, we include class attributes, method parameters, and local variables. So lambdas are inline functions plus closures all in one. We'll just call these things *lambdas* from this point on.

What problem do lambdas solve?

All this talk of closures and inline functions is fairly abstract. Perhaps, this construct is better understood by demonstrating the problem it solves. We don't even need to discuss functional programming; lambdas have practical uses even if transported into the realm of the object-oriented paradigm. If nothing else, lambdas facilitate the programming of *behavior-as-data*. This is the idea of passing behavior to methods, variables, and attributes. Sure it's possible to do this in classic Java, but not without terms and conditions. Consider the following code snippet:

```
public boolean isBalanceSufficient(Account account, double amount) {
    logAccess(account);
    boolean isBalanceSufficient = account.getBalance() - amount > 0;

    if (!isBalanceSufficient) {
        // It would be nice to let the caller vary this condition
        if (account.getCreditRating() > 700) {
            isBalanceSufficient = true;
            alertOverdraw(account);
        }

    }

    return isBalanceSufficient;
}
```

The method *isBalanceSufficient()* checks whether or not the given account, represented by *account*, has sufficient funds to make a withdrawal. If it does, *true* is returned. Otherwise, it checks whether or not the account holder is "good for it". In banker's terminology, the bank can allow an overdraft and lend the money if the client has a good credit rating. So the method will still return *true* if the credit risk is tolerable. One line of code handles this exception case in the middle of the method:

```
if (account.getCreditRating() > 700)
```

The problem arises if we need to vary the condition for granting exemptions. We would like to let the caller decide *how* to grant exemptions. Because the *if-condition* is sandwiched between two blocks of code, it would be awkward to split the method in three parts. A *poor man*'s solution would look like this:

```
// Part 1
public boolean isBalanceSufficient(Account account, double amount) {
    logAccess(account);
    return account.getBalance() - amount > 0;
}

// Part 2
public void doOverdraft(Account account, double amount) {
    alertOverdraw(account);
}
```

```
// Part 3
if (!isBalanceSufficient(anAccount, anAmount)) {
    // Caller can now vary the condition and control the flow
    if (anAccount.getCreditRating() > 700) {
        doOverdraft(anAccount, anAmount);
    }
}
```

The two portions of code above and below the condition have been refactored into their own methods and the caller now coordinates the flow. The caller can now vary the condition in case of an insufficient balance. This solution is not elegant in the least. The problem is exacerbated with cut-and-paste duplication throughout the code base if a withdrawal call is made from multiple points. Now, every time we need to find out if the balance is sufficient, we end up with a lot more code.

In object-oriented orthodoxy, the prescribed solution would be to create a new interface that allows the *if-condition* to be specified by the caller and passed as a method parameter. Here's one incarnation of this idea:

```
public interface Exemptable {
    boolean isExempt(Account account);
}
```

The *isExempt()* method allows the implementer to decide whether or not to grant an exemption for the given account. Incorporating the new interface, we can refactor the original method like this:

```
public boolean isBalanceSufficient(Account account,
                                   double amount, Exemptable ex) {
    logAccess(account);
    boolean isBalanceSufficient = account.getBalance() - amount > 0;

    if (!isBalanceSufficient) {
        // Now, we can let the caller vary the condition
        if (ex.isExempt(account)) {
            isBalanceSufficient = true;
            alertOverdraw(account);
        }
    }
    return isBalanceSufficient;
}
```

The caller now has a way to set the condition and control how exemptions are granted. We've created injectable behavior right in the middle of the method. For example, we can create an anonymous class of *Exemptable()*:

```
// Create an anonymous class
isBalanceSufficient(anAccount, anAmount,
    new Exemptable() {
            @Override
            public boolean isExempt(Account account) {
                return account.getCreditRating() > 700;
            }
    });
```

Here, a credit score of 700 or more (e.g., an implementation for a Canadian bank) is the criteria used to determine whether or not an account is given an exemption. This can now be tailored for any credit score system in the world or any other scheme banks can plot.

So what's wrong with this tried and tested technique? There are, in fact, several problems:

- **Verbosity**: Java has long been criticized for being too verbose. Even with this anonymous class—the most concise way to implement interfaces in Java— many lines of coded are needed to get to the crux of the issue. There is only one statement we really care about:

    ```
    return account.getCreditRating() > 700;
    ```

    Yet, we needed to:
    1. Create an *Exemptable* interface.
    2. Create a new *Exemptable* object.
    3. Override the *isExempt()* method.
    4. Include the *@Override* annotation.
    5. Test the condition on the account.
    6. Return the value.
    7. Include all the braces and parentheses.

    That's a lot of overhead for a simple account condition test!

- **Boilerplate code**: If we need to keep on defining anonymous classes throughout the code base, each with subtle differences, the result is boilerplate implementations, usually a sign of code smell. But in Java, it's difficult to improve upon this.

What we really wanted was to just pass raw behavior to *isBalanceSufficient()* but instead, Java forced us to pass a class construct. Granted, we used an anonymous class to blunt the pain but, as we saw, there was still too much overhead. Is there a way to define only the essence (the *if-statement*) and do away with the overhead? Let's see how lambdas can help.

Introducing the Java lambda

Let's start by discussing the lambda form. In their most basic incarnation, lambdas have the following three parts:

```
            1                       2           3
(Parameter declaration)            ->    { Lambda body }
```

Just like method parameters, lambdas can have parameters enclosed within parentheses. The lambda body defines behavior and is enclosed within curly braces. Java 8 introduces the -> operator as a new syntactical addition to the language, one of several more to come. It separates the parameters from the body.

Incidentally, lambdas, like methods, can have any number of parameters and need not return anything. Parameterless lambdas have the following format:

```
            () -> { Lambda body }
```

As well, lambda bodies can be empty:

```
            () -> { }
```

Lambdas have been introduced into Java with great care. Java is a strongly and statically-typed system so lambdas need to somehow fit in. When behavior is passed around, what is its type? It can't just be code floating around—it has to fit into Java's type system so that it can have some sort of handle. Java's answer is to tie lambdas to interfaces. In fact, all lambdas are backed by a specific interface. When instantiated at runtime, they become full blown objects—just like anonymous classes or any other class for that matter.

Let's return to our *Exemptable* problem with lambdas in mind.

The Exemptable lambda

Our re-factored example using a lambda looks like this:

```
// Our very first Java lambda!
Exemptable ex = (Account acc) ->
                {return acc.getCreditRating() > 700;};
isBalanceSufficient(anAccount, anAmount, ex);
```

If nothing else, we have replaced eight lines with their semantic two-liner equivalent. Granted, we cheated by using a more compact coding style in the lambda example, but you'll see that as we re-factor this code further, lambdas truly enable compactness.

There are only two lines of code in that snippet but there is a lot going on behind the scenes. Our lambda fits the mold:

```
Parameter declaration                               Body

   (Account acc)          ->      {return acc.getCreditRating() > 700;};
```

The lambda conforms to the *Exemptable* interface because its signature, comprising of the parameter declaration and return type, is compatible with the *Exemptable's isExempt()* method. Notice that our lambda does not explicitly implement the *Exemptable* interface in order to declare to which interface it conforms. Instead, the Java compiler can infer that the lambda is an *Exemptable* implementation because it conforms to that target interface. Specifically, the compiler uses this logic to determine suitability:

- Is *Exemptable* a functional interface declaring exactly one method?[2]
- Does the lambda have the same number of parameters as the *Exemptable.isExempt()* method?

---

[2] Functional interfaces are explained in the next chapter.

- Are the lambda's parameters compatible with *isExempt()*?
- Is the lambda's return type compatible with *isExempt()*?
- If exceptions are thrown, are they allowed by *isExempt()*?

Since the answer to all these questions is *yes*, the lambda is compatible. Inference is one of the great features of lambdas in that it really promotes the notion of defining behavior on the fly. Functional programming is a behavior-centric paradigm and lambdas are designed to work in this context.

As an additional point, our lambda was declared and assigned to the local variable *ex* but that was for code clarity—not to help out the compiler in its inference magic. The compiler relies solely on these five questions to determine suitability as an *Exemptable* provider.

When *isBalanceSufficient()* is executed, an object is created out of the lambda expression. From the perspective of this method, it receives an instance of *Exemptable* and does not know or care that the code originated from a lambda. Its method can be invoked, it can be passed along to other methods, it can be assigned to other variables, and it will be garbage collected when out of scope. Even *equals()*, *getClass()*, *hashCode()*, *notify()*, *notifyAll()*, *toString()*, and *wait()* can be invoked.

As much as the compiler is performing a good deal of inference, the code is intentionally written in the most verbose way. It's actually quite verbose for functional programming standards. The compiler can infer a great deal more and this translates into less code for developers. We can remove the following excesses:

```
Exemptable ex = (Account acc) ->
                {return acc.getCreditRating() > 700;};
isBalanceSufficient(anAccount, anAmount, ex);
```

In this second version, the return keyword, the braces, and the first semi-colon have all been removed. This is because our lambda contains only one statement and can be re-written this way:

```
Exemptable ex = (Account acc) -> acc.getCreditRating() > 700;
isBalanceSufficient(anAccount, anAmount, ex);
```

Single-statement lambdas, such as the one in the previous example, are known as *lambda expressions*. Java 8 grants lambda expressions syntactical privileges: they need not contain curly braces nor *return* keywords. This does not apply to *lambda blocks*, which are lambdas with more than one statement. This is an important privilege because lambda expressions are quite common in functional programming. They enable a very concise style of programming where lambda expressions are passed to functions. We'll see many instances where lambda expressions can be used with the new Java 8 libraries.

As good as this may be, we're not quite finished. We can remove even more excess to create an even more fluid style:

```
Exemptable ex = (Account acc) -> acc.getCreditRating() > 700;
isBalanceSufficient(anAccount, anAmount, ex);
```

In this third revision, we've stripped off the parameter type, in this case *Account*, resulting in:

```
Exemptable ex = (acc) -> acc.getCreditRating() > 700;
isBalanceSufficient(anAccount, anAmount, ex);
```

In fact, the Java compiler can usually determine the lambda's parameter type automatically, even for multi-parameter lambdas. Parentheses surrounding the parameters can be removed as well:

```
Exemptable ex = (acc) -> acc.getCreditRating() > 700;
isBalanceSufficient(anAccount, anAmount, ex);
```

Yielding this style that should be the favored style for all lambdas, except in cases where the compiler cannot infer the parameter type.

```
Exemptable ex = acc -> acc.getCreditRating() > 700;
isBalanceSufficient(anAccount, anAmount, ex);
```

There is one final improvement that can be made. As previously alluded to, the local variable *ex* does not help the compiler determine that this is an *Exemptable* lambda. The compiler figures that out automatically based on signature matching. We can remove the entire line and directly define the lambda as the third parameter of *isBalanceSufficient()*:

```
Exemptable ex = account -> account.getCreditRating() > 700;
isBalanceSufficient(anAccount, anAmount,
                    account -> account.getCreditRating() > 700);
```

This final incarnation of the credit score lambda fits as a third parameter of the *isBalanceSufficient()* method:

```
isBalanceSufficient(anAccount, anAmount,
                    account -> account.getCreditRating() > 700);
```

Java developers are accustomed to looking at method parameters and supplying instances compatible with the expected types. On the other hand, when defining lambdas on the fly, such as in this example, we must define a lambda whose signature matches the target type, and this cannot be determined without digging into the interface's method. Lambdas are deceivingly simple and require a change in habit.

Our final implementation was a far cry from the original implementation, which required four lines of code, plus the accompanying braces, parentheses, semi-colons, and return keyword.

Wrap up

Lambdas really do promote a more fluid style of programming, but there is much more to lambdas than just conciseness. They are a disruptive force in Java, as they will profoundly change your way of thinking about code. The very basic idea of cutting code into small pieces and passing behavior-only constructs is at the very core of functional programming. The lambda is the vehicle that allows code to be structured in this way. We are only scratching the surface. In the next chapter, we'll continue with our tour of the new Java 8 syntax.

Key points

- The terms *lambda* and *closure* have been used interchangeably in the Java world but are in fact distinct. In Java, a lambda is also a closure because it is not only an inline function but it also contains all of its surrounding context.

- Lambdas facilitate the behavior-as-data construct and are much less verbose than anonymous classes.

- Although lambdas do not implement interfaces, they must conform to one.

- A number of factors determine suitability, including the parameter types and return types of the target interface.

- Lambda expressions are single-statement lambda bodies. Lambdas blocks are multi-statement lambda bodies.

- Java treats lambda expressions favorably, allowing for code shorthands such as the elimination of braces, semi-colons, and *return* keywords.

Chapter 3:
Functional, default, & reference methods

Functional interfaces

We continue with the anatomy of lambdas in Java. Since interfaces are the backbone of lambdas, they have acquired greater prominence in Java 8. Many changes were made to interfaces to better accommodate lambdas, which we'll explore in this chapter. The first is the concept of a *functional interface.* Functional interfaces are a special type of interface against which lambdas are defined. They must declare exactly one method, which is to be implemented by the lambda. This is sometimes called the single abstract method rule or SAM rule. It is illegal to declare more than one method and this can be enforced at compilation time with the new annotation named *@FunctionalInterface*.

In our previous example, we created the *Exemptable* interface to work with our lambda. The *Exemptable* interface was technically not a functional one because it did not use the annotation, but it was legal nonetheless. Now that we know better, we can add the annotation:

```java
@FunctionalInterface
public interface Exemptable {
    boolean isExempt(Account account);
}
```

Now we have a real functional interface. The annotation allows us to communicate our intent clearly. If we added a second method, compilation would fail:

```java
@FunctionalInterface
public interface Exemptable {
    boolean isExempt(Account account);

    // Fails compilation because functional interfaces can
    // only declare one abstract method
    boolean anotherExemption(Account account);
}
```

This allows us to add more compile-time checks in our code. While it is not illegal to omit the *@FunctionalInterface* annotation, it is nevertheless standard practice and highly recommended to always specify it.

As a side note, in functional parlance, *isExempt()* is a function rather than a method because it specifies behavior only with no residual state. But the Java community does not make this distinction and continues to use the term *method* even within the context of a functional interface. We will respect this tradition.

Using functional interfaces

Let's revisit the original *isBalanceSufficient()* method and make some additional changes. Suppose we wanted to add some other injectable behavior. For example, whenever the bank granted an exemption, we would like to give the caller the opportunity to do something extra; for example, we can log the fact that an exemption was granted, raise an alarm, or do anything else we can imagine.

We can create a new *AccountExemptionHandler* functional interface:

```
@FunctionalInterface
public interface AccountExemptionHandler {
    public void onAccountExempted(Account account);
}
```

And refactor the code that uses it:

```
public boolean isBalanceSufficient(
    Account account, double amount, Exemptable exemptable,
    AccountExemptionHandler handler) {
    logAccess(account);
    boolean isBalanceSufficient = account.getBalance() - amount > 0;

    if (!isBalanceSufficient) {
        if (exemptable.isExempt(account)) {
            isBalanceSufficient = true;

            // Give caller the opportunity to do something extra
            handler.onAccountExempted(account);
        }
    }

    return isBalanceSufficient;
}
```

Suppose, for example, that we would like to print the account information every time an exemption has been granted. Let's see how you might implement this. Again, you can start with an anonymous class of *AccountExemptionHandler* to ease your entry into Java 8. Using an anonymous class would yield this kind of code:

```
// Anonymous class implementation of AccountExemptionHandler
AccountExemptionHandler  anonymousAccountExemptionHandler  =
    new AccountExemptionHandler () {
  @Override
  public void onAccountExempted(Account account) {
    System.out.println(account);
  }
};
```

However, these training wheels should be removed because lambdas are a better tool for the job. We can remove the entire overhead that anonymous classes force upon us:

```
isBalanceSufficient
   (account, amount, acc -> acc.getCreditRating() > 700,
    new AccountExemptionHandler () {
      @Override
      public void accountExemptionHandler (Account account) {
        System.out.println(account);
      }
   });
```

...and use lambdas instead:

```
isBalanceSufficient
   (account, amount,
    acc -> acc.getCreditRating() > 700,
    acc -> System.out.println(account));
```

As before, we can fully minimize the code footprint of the lambda by using the expression form and removing the *Account* type definition, the return keyword, and the braces. As concise as this already is, these types of lambdas can be streamlined even further. Notice that this lambda is only acting as a bridge between the *isBalanceSufficient()* and *println()* methods, passing along the *account* parameter. It has no additional logic of its own to add. In such cases, we can use a brand new concept in Java 8.

Introducing method references

When a lambda is only bridging two methods, something that occurs frequently in Java functional programming, we can use method references instead. Method references are a brand new Java 8 construct that allows us to take coding shortcuts. They can be conceptualized as bridging mechanisms that simply pass along the lambda parameters to another method. Rather than writing the bridge code, we can use method references like this:

```
isBalanceSufficient
   (account, amount,
    acc -> acc.getCreditRating() > 700,
    // The lambda has been replaced by a method reference
    System.out::println);
```

In this case, that method is calling *println()* from *PrintStream* (via *System.out*). Since the lambda in the previous example did nothing but pass along the *acc* parameter to the *println(),* the method reference provides a convenient shorthand. This works because, looking at the call flow, *isBalanceSufficient()* expects an *AccountExemptionHandler* type whose *onAccountExempted()* method expects an *Account* and returns a void. Since *println* has a signature compatible with *onAccountExempted()*, it can be used as a proxy and specified as a method reference. We can visualize this concept better with this diagram:

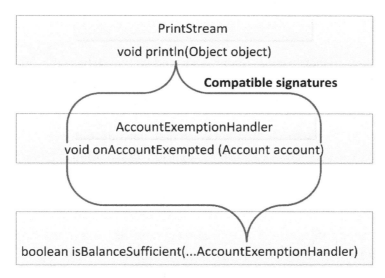

Figure 3: Method reference matching

There are two particularly interesting things about this example. First, the Java compiler automatically links the *Account* parameter in *AccountExemptionHandler* *.onAccountExempted(Account)* to the object parameter in *println(Object)*. Second, the compiler is led to believe that *println()* is a suitable implementer of the *AccountExemptionHandler* interface, even though it does not explicitly implement that interface. Again, just like with lambdas, the magic is performed through signature matching. The signature of method *println()* declares an *Object* parameter and has a *void* return. This happens to be compatible with the *onAccountExempted()* method defined in *AccountExemptionHandler*. The two signatures match and are bound together. This is a powerful concept. Method references remove the need to spell out how to connect *account* from *isBalanceSufficient()* to the input parameter of *println()*. They bring Java one tiny step closer to being a declarative language—a key piece of functional programming. In the above example, we don't code the steps to perform the *println()*: that would be imperative thinking. Instead, we just say that we want a *println()*.

You can use method references to refer to any method, whether your own or 3rd party, adhering to the same method visibility rules that would apply to traditional method invocation. As well, they can refer to methods having any number of parameters. You never specify parameters in method references as the compiler will automatically match the method reference with the functional interface. In the above example, *AccountExemptionHandler* has one parameter, and so it matches with *println()* (also one parameter). Had *AccountExemptionHandler* required two parameters, the syntax would have been identical, provided the referred method signature was compatible.

Method references can seem a little tricky at first. Java developers are accustomed to seeing a direct link from method call to method body. Method references add an intermediary step. When analyzing a call flow with method references, you must first understand what signature the target method expects, via its functional interface. Then, you must ensure that the caller is passing a signature-compatible method reference. Lambdas also require this same kind of mental gymnastics, but at least developers have been exposed to this exercise through anonymous classes. Method references are something completely new to Java. With time, this will become second nature.

Method references as bridges

Note that method references only work as lambda substitutes when the lambda body does nothing more than call another method passing along parameters. Consider the *Exemptable* lambda body that doesn't fit the mold:

```
isBalanceSufficient
  (account, amount,
    // Cannot use a method reference because it's not a bridge
    acc -> acc.getCreditRating() > 700, System.out::println);
```

However, an interesting aspect of method references is that we can create an intermediate method that will contain the credit rating check. We can define the static method *defaultExemption()*:

```
// From the Banker class
public static boolean defaultExemption(Account account) {
    return account.getCreditRating() > 700;
}
```

And refer to it via a method reference:

```
isBalanceSufficient
    (account, amount,
    // Refer to a static method within the Banker class.
    // Replaces:  a -> Banker::defaultExemption (a)
    Banker::defaultExemption,
    System.out::println);
```

Now, the method *defaultExemption()* matches the signature of *Exemptable.isExempt()*: it takes an *account* and returns a *boolean* type. This is exactly what the *isExempt()* method requires.

This example highlights two important points. First, method references can substitute any lambda block or expression if we're willing to write intermediary methods when necessary. This can make the code more compact. Second, method references used this way allow code to be labelled and reused. For example, *defaultExemption* can be referred to anywhere *isBalanceSufficient()* is used.

Having multiple ways of expressing behavior-as-data gives us choices, but what is the strategy for choosing between lambda expressions, blocks, or method references? As a general guideline, use a method reference whenever your lambda is simply acting as a bridge. In fact, your editor will identify lambdas that act as bridges and suggest switching to method references. If you need to do more, use a lambda expression whenever possible. Otherwise, use a lambda block but factor out the method for longer, reusable blocks and use a method reference to refer to it.

Method reference varieties

The code example above used the method reference *Banker::defaultExemption*. This is an illustration of a static method reference. However, there are actually six different types of method references in Java 8. These are: *static, instance, super, constructor, generic type constructor,* and *array constructor.* Let's look at what each of these does.

Static	*Class::method* Used to refer to a static method of a class.
Instance	*instanceVariable::method* Used to refer to an instance method of a class.
Super	super::*method* Used to refer to an instance method found in a parent class.
Constructor	*Class*::new Used to refer to a constructor of a class.
Generic type constructors	*Class<Type>*::new Used to refer to a constructor of a generic class.
Array constructors	*Class*[]::new Used to refer to a constructor of an array.

Let's continue with our *Banker* example to demonstrate the use for all types of method references. The entire *Banker* class is shown here:

```java
public class Banker extends SuperBanker {
    public boolean isBalanceSufficient
        (Account account, double amount,
         Exemptable exemptable, AccountExemptionHandler handler) {
        // Details omitted…
    }

    private void logAccess(Account account) {
        System.out.println("Account was accessed: " +
                                account.getAccountId());
    }

    public List<Account> makeDefaultAccounts
        (int count, AccountCreator accountCreator,
         ListCreator<List<Account>> listCreator) {
        List<Account> returnList = listCreator.create();
        for (int index=0; index < count; ++index) {
            returnList.add(accountCreator.create("default"));
        }

        return returnList;
    }

    public Account[] makeArrayDefaultAccounts
        (int count, AccountCreator accountCreator,
         AccountArrayCreator accountArrayCreator) {
        Account[] returnList = accountArrayCreator.create(count);

        for (int index=0; index < count; ++index) {
            returnList[index] = accountCreator.create("default");
        }

        return returnList;
    }

    public static boolean defaultExemption(Account account) {
        return account.getCreditRating() > 700;
    }

    public void instanceAccountExemptionHandler(Account account) {
        System.out.println("Account: " + account.getAccountId() +
                                " was given an exemption");
    }
```

```
    public void runTheBank(Account account, double amount) {
        isBalanceSufficient
            (account, amount,
            // Static method reference
            Banker::defaultExemption,
            // Instance method reference
            this::instanceAccountExemptionHandler );
    }
}
```

We've already seen static method references, now let's look at an example of an instance method reference. The class method *instanceAccountExemptionHandler()* is created and called from within *runTheBank()*. Notice that it uses *this::* to refer to it because it is called from within the same class. Had the method been called from outside of the class, it would have had this form instead: *instanceVariable::method.* For example:

```
Banker bankerInstance = new Banker();
bankerInstance.isBalanceSufficient
            (account, amount,
            Banker::defaultExemption,
            bankerInstance::instanceAccountExemptionHandler);
```

A variant of the instance method reference is the *super* method reference. Here, we use the *super* keyword to refer to an instance method of the parent class.

```
isBalanceSufficient
    (account, amount,
    Banker::defaultExemption,
    // Refer to super AccountExemptionHandler in the parent class
    super::superAccountExemptionHandler);
```

Now, the *superAccountExemptionHandler()* method is used instead.

Constructor method references variants

Java 8 allows the use of constructor, generic constructor, as well as array constructor references. These are useful to declaratively program object construction. We start with constructor methods. To demonstrate, we create three new functional interfaces: *AccountCreator, ListCreator,* and *AccountArrayCreator.*

```java
@FunctionalInterface
public interface AccountCreator {
    Account create(String accountId);
}


@FunctionalInterface
public interface ListCreator<T extends List> {
    T create();
}


@FunctionalInterface
public interface AccountArrayCreator {
    Account[] create(int value);
}
```

Notice the *makeDefaultAccounts()* method in *Banker*:

```java
public List<Account> makeDefaultAccounts
    (int count, AccountCreator accountCreator,
     ListCreator<List<Account>> listCreator) {
    List<Account> returnList = listCreator.create();
    for (int index=0; index < count; ++index) {
        returnList.add(accountCreator.create("default"));
    }

    return returnList;
}
```

This method will create a number of default *Accounts* and return them in a list. Using lambdas, we call the method like this:

```java
makeDefaultAccounts
    (10,
    // These do nothing more than bridge to other methods
    id -> new Account(id),
    () -> new LinkedList<Account>());
```

Since these lambdas are only acting as bridges to constructors, it makes sense to use constructor and generic constructor method references instead:

```
makeDefaultAccounts
   (10,
    Account::new,                     // Constructor reference
    LinkedList<Account>::new); // Generic constructor reference
```

Array constructor references are also useful. Notice the *makeArrayDefaultAccounts()* method in *Banker*:

```
public Account[] makeArrayDefaultAccounts
   (int count, AccountCreator accountCreator,
    AccountArrayCreator accountArrayCreator) {
    Account[] returnList = accountArrayCreator.create(count);

    for (int index=0; index < count; ++index) {
        returnList[index] = accountCreator.create("default");
    }

    return returnList;
}
```

Without array constructor references, we would call *makeArrayDefaultAccounts()* this way:

```
makeArrayDefaultAccounts
   (10, Account::new, size -> new Account[size]);
```

We can do better with array constructor references:

```
makeArrayDefaultAccounts(10, Account::new, Account[]::new);
```

Constructor method references are useful when the methods called are in control of object creation but need to be told which constructor to use. In this case, the caller needs only to specify which constructor to use. They will come in handy in the functional libraries we'll explore in later chapters.

Custom vs. standard functional interfaces

So far, we've created our own custom functional interfaces. They included *Exemptable, AccountExemptionHandler, AccountCreator, ListCreator,* and *AccountArrayCreator.* However, it was a purely academic exercise useful only in demonstrating how method references work. The reality is that you will rarely need to create such interfaces. To simplify every day programming and eliminate the proliferation of trivial interfaces, JDK 8 ships with a starter kit of 40-something basic functional interfaces. These are used primarily by Java's own libraries, such as the Collections library, but are public and available for your own code. In fact, all five of our custom functional interfaces could have been replaced by the standard functional interfaces. Only in rare cases should you roll your own. We'll cover these standard functional interfaces in chapter 5.

Anonymous classes vs. lambdas

Now that Java 8 offers a better construct to define behavior on the fly, do anonymous classes still have a place in the developer's toolkit? They do. First, they offer an easier transition into the world of functional programming. Java 8 permits the use of anonymous classes as incarnations of functional interfaces. This means that a naïve Java developer can continue to use anonymous classes whenever a method parameter expects a functional interface type. In fact, a good Java IDE will do the thinking for you and offer to convert your anonymous class into a lambda. If you're not sure how to code a lambda, start with an anonymous class then upgrade to a lambda. Think of anonymous classes as functional programming on training wheels.

Beyond their use as a learning tool, anonymous classes are still required for an object-oriented programming style, which Java still endorses. Lambdas, on the other hand, are meant to be behavior-only constructs that fit the functional programming philosophy. Thus you cannot blindly substitute all your anonymous functions in your existing code base with lambdas. Consider the design of *ObjectOrientedTimedRunnable*:

```
public abstract class ObjectOrientedTimedRunnable implements
    Runnable {
    private long executionDuration;

    @Override
    public abstract void run();

    public final void runTimed() throws InterruptedException {
        long startTime = System.currentTimeMillis();

        Thread thread = new Thread(this);
        thread.start();
        thread.join();

        executionDuration = System.currentTimeMillis() - startTime;
    }

    public final long getExecutionDuration() {
        return executionDuration;
    }
}
```

ObjectOrientedTimedRunnable is an abstract class used to time the execution of a *Runnable* block of code. As a client of this class, you provide an implementation of the *Runnable* interface and call *runTimed()*:

```
ObjectOrientedTimedRunnable runner =
    new ObjectOrientedTimedRunnable() {
        @Override
        public void run() {
            // do something you want to time!
        }
    };

runner.runTimed();
System.out.println("Time: " + runner.getExecutionDuration());
```

This will execute the *Runnable* code inside a thread and preserve the execution duration. The result is fetched in a separate call using *getExecutionDuration()*. The trouble here is that *ObjectOrientedTimedRunnable*, as its name suggests, was designed in an object-oriented conversational style. We are thus forced to use an anonymous class because:

1. State is kept between creation, *runTimed()*, and *getExecutionDuration()*. Lambdas forbid state.
2. Lambdas must be backed by functional interfaces. *ObjectOrientedTimedRunnable* is an abstract class. These cannot be functional interfaces.
3. This abstract class also defines an additional public method. Lambdas can only be backed by functional interfaces, which allow only one method to implement.

Can we re-code this example as a lambda? We can, but we must first address all three points and re-design it in a functional style. The first step is to remove all states from the abstract class:

```
public abstract class StatelessTimedRunnable implements Runnable {
    public abstract void run();

    public long runTimed() throws InterruptedException {
        System.out.println("Running StatelessTimedRunnable");
        long startTime = System.currentTimeMillis();

        Thread thread = new Thread(this);
        thread.start();
        thread.join();

        return System.currentTimeMillis() - startTime;
    }
}
```

StatelessTimedRunnable is a stateless incarnation that no longer keeps state. It returns the duration in *runTimed()* instead. This yields more concise code because we can time the method and get the duration in one statement. The bigger problem is that we still can't use a lambda because we still have an abstract class with two methods. We can try to convert *StatelessTimedRunnable* into a functional interface, but what about *runTimed()*? We cannot move a method body inside an interface. Can Java 8 help?

Default methods

This may come as a shock to Java developers but interfaces can now define behavior! These are called *default methods*. Default methods define behavior that can be overridden by a sub-interface or class. They are marked as such with the keyword *default* prepended to the method declaration:

```
default void doSomething(Object takeSomething) {
    // do something
}
```

Default methods can be used in functional or regular interfaces and there can be any number of them inside an interface. Within the scope of a functional interface, default methods are not considered abstract and therefore don't count towards the single abstract method rule.

We can now convert *StatelessTimedRunnable* into a functional interface and use default methods:

```
@FunctionalInterface
public interface FunctionalTimedRunnable extends Runnable {
    // Wow! Interfaces can now define behavior!
    default long runTimed() throws InterruptedException {
        printInterfaceName("FunctionalTimedRunnable");
        long startTime = System.currentTimeMillis();

        Thread thread = new Thread(this);
        thread.start();
        thread.join();
        return System.currentTimeMillis() - startTime;
    }

    default void launchTest() throws InterruptedException {
        System.out.println("This thread executed for: " + runTimed()
                        + " ms.");
    }

    default void printInterfaceName(String interfaceName) {
        System.out.println("Running " + interfaceName);
    }
}
```

We now have our first functional incarnation of *TimedRunnable* via *FunctionalTimedRunnable* using a functional interface. As well, *runTimed()* has been converted to a default method. We've also added a utility method named *launchTest()* to print a formatted message and another named *printInterfaceName()*. Just like a regular method, *launchTest()* can be invoked from any other default method. Additionally, default methods can be overridden by sub-interfaces and the usual Java polymorphism takes effect. Finally, default methods can only be public or package-private, just like regular interface methods, and they cannot be final.

We can now implement *FunctionalTimedRunnable* as a lambda and do away with the original anonymous class:

```
public static void testFunctionalTimedRunnable()
    throws InterruptedException {
    FunctionalTimedRunnable timedRunnable =
        () -> {/* Do something*/};
    timedRunnable.launchTest();
}
```

We now have a more interesting usage of the *FunctionalTimedRunnable* interface. The static method *testFunctionalTimedRunnable()* defines a lambda that contains the code to run inside a thread. Then, we simply invoke the default method *launchTest()* and this will time the execution of the lambda body.

Default methods offer a brand new way to design objects. They were born out of necessity in making the Collections library backward compatible. This library was modeled as a deep hierarchy of interfaces, including prominent members such as *Collection*, *List*, *Map*, and *Set*. They needed to be enriched to make lambdas truly useful for everyday programming. After all, the Collections library is where Java becomes functional. But given Java's longstanding policy on respecting backward compatibility, refactoring the hierarchy to better support lambdas was out of the question. Understandably, this would have broken all existing Java deployments and countless 3rd party libraries extending the Collections hierarchy. Instead, the language architects opted for the *default* construct, an option friendly to backward compatibility. Adding default methods to existing interfaces only enriches them without breaking contracts. This applies to classes that use the Collection libraries as well as those that extend the classes and interfaces. We'll discuss the changes to the Collections library in chapter 5.

But default methods are more than just a crutch to preserve legacy Java: they aid you in thinking functionally. A functional interface with default methods is a pure behavior-only construct. It cannot hold state. This aligns your thinking with functional programming and allows you to take advantage of what the programming model has to offer. Default methods will have a big impact on 3rd API design in the Java community—just like they've had in the standard JDK libraries.

Functional interface extension

What happens if we need to add behavior via inheritance? Functional interfaces can be extended like any other interface. For example, we can add more sophistication to the calculation. Here, *AverageTimedRunnable* executes the runnable five times and returns an average, but it does so by building upon *FunctionalTimedRunnable* through extension:

```
@FunctionalInterface
public interface AverageTimedRunnable extends
   FunctionalTimedRunnable {
   default long runTimed() throws InterruptedException {
       printInterfaceName("AverageTimedRunnable");
       long timeSum = 0;

       for (int count = 0; count < 5; ++count) {
           timeSum +=
               FunctionalTimedRunnable.super.runTimed();
       }

       return Math.round(timeSum / 5);
   }
}
```

Notice that *AverageTimedRunnable* calls two super methods differently. First, *printInterfaceName()* is called like any other method, but *runTimed()* is called like this:

```
FunctionalTimedRunnable.super.runTimed();
```

Since the *runTimed()* method has been redefined in this interface, the use of *super()* is required to invoke the parent implementation and necessary to resolve ambiguity; otherwise, we get a recursive call. However, this form only works to access default methods from directly extended interfaces. In this example, *super* is used to access *runTimed()* from *FunctionalTimedRunnable*; it could not use *super* to access a default method in *Runnable* (if it had one) because *Runnable* is not directly extended. However, any non-overridden default method can be accessed without the *super* keyword. The invocation of *printInterfaceName("AverageTimedRunnable")* is an example.

In the above example, *runTimed()* overrode the parent implementation. But default methods introduce a brand new problem in Java. Since multiple interface inheritance is possible, what happens when a default method is inherited via two parents? This could happen, for example, if we enrich our design to add a new interface, *MedianTimedRunnable*, which also extends *FunctionalTimedRunnable* and implements its own *runTimed()*:

```
@FunctionalInterface
public interface MedianTimedRunnable extends
   FunctionalTimedRunnable {
    default long runTimed() throws InterruptedException {
        printInterfaceName("MedianTimedRunnable ");
        final int sampleSize = 5;
        ArrayList<Long> longs = new ArrayList<>(sampleSize);

        for (int count = 0; count < sampleSize; ++count) {
           longs.add(
               FunctionalTimedRunnable.super.runTimed());
        }

        Collections.sort(longs);
        return longs.get(sampleSize / 2);
    }
}
```

Also, we add a *SmartTimedRunnable* that extends both *AverageTimedRunnable* and *MedianTimedRunnable*:

```
@FunctionalInterface
public interface SmartTimedRunnable extends
  AverageTimedRunnable, MedianTimedRunnable {
    public default long runTimed() throws InterruptedException {
        printInterfaceName("SmartTimedRunnable");
        long averageElapsedTime =
           AverageTimedRunnable.super.runTimed();

        // Choose average time if less than 1 second
        return averageElapsedTime < 1000 ?
           averageElapsedTime:
               MedianTimedRunnable.super.runTimed();
    }
}
```

However, we now have introduced the infamous "diamond problem" to our class design as shown in Figure 4. *SmartTimedRunnable* inherits *runTimed()* from two different lineages: *AverageTimedRunnable* and *MedianTimedRunnable*.

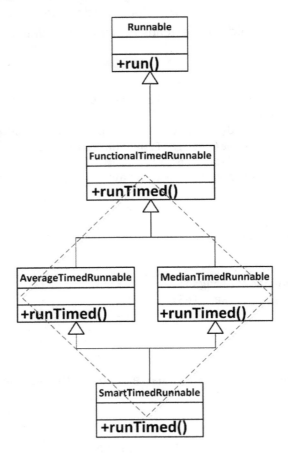

Figure 4: "Diamond" inheritance

In this example, *SmartTimedRunnable* explicitly chose which version of *runTimed()* it wanted. But Java 8 has three rules for resolving conflicts brought upon by multiple inheritance when ambiguous:

1. Overrides from concrete classes take precedence over interface default methods.
2. Sub-interface methods take precedence over super-interface methods.
3. Explicitness takes precedence over inference.

Basically, you let the Java compiler resolve ambiguities using the first two rules. If that doesn't fit your needs, you resolve ambiguities through class name qualifiers.

Java's stance on eschewing multiple class inheritance was touted as an improvement over C++ in the early days. The knock on multiple class inheritance was the diamond problem specifically. This is because in addition to inheriting behavior from multiple lineages, state would also be inherited and had to be managed properly across the hierarchy. For example, with state inheritance, *AverageTimedRunnable* and *MedianTimedRunnable* could each manage state inherited from *FunctionalTimedRunnable* in a conflicting manner. Granted that Java 8 will somewhat complexify interface inheritance with default methods, the larger problem of state management is avoided because there is no state in interfaces. In short, just apply these three simple rules to resolve default method inheritance problems.

Static method references

We just showed that it is entirely possible to port a program designed with an object-oriented mindset into a functional one. We got rid of conversational state, an impediment to functional programming, introduced functional interfaces, and used default methods as functions. But we could also have used static methods to achieve similar goals. Java 8 allows functional interfaces to contain static methods as well.

Static methods in functional interfaces have the same syntax as regular interfaces. Like their default method counterparts, there can be any number of static methods in functional interfaces but they must still adhere to the single abstract method rule. Let's adapt our timed runnable example using static methods instead of default ones:

```
@FunctionalInterface
public interface StaticTimedRunnable extends Runnable {
    static long runTimed(StaticTimedRunnable timedRunnable)
        throws InterruptedException {
        printInterfaceName("StaticTimedRunnable");
        long startTime = System.currentTimeMillis();

        Thread thread = new Thread(timedRunnable);
        thread.start();
        thread.join();
        return System.currentTimeMillis() - startTime;
    }

    static void launchTest(StaticTimedRunnable runnable)
        throws InterruptedException {
        System.out.println("This thread executed for: " +
                                    runTimed(runnable) + " ms.");
    }

    static void printInterfaceName(String interfaceName) {
        System.out.println("Running " + interfaceName);
    }
}
```

The code is similar to *FunctionalTimedRunnable* except that the method *launchTest()* now needs to be given a *StaticTimedRunnable* as a parameter. This is because as a static interface, it does not have access to the *this* since static methods—just like regular classes—have no access to instance methods.

In this example, *StaticTimedRunnable* inherits *run()* from *Runnable* so it conforms to the single abstract method rule. Since a thread requiring a *Runnable* is needed in *runTimed(),* *StaticTimedRunnable* extends from *Runnable*. We can use *StaticTimedRunnable* like this:

```
StaticTimedRunnable.launchTest(() -> {/* do something */ });
```

Think of *StaticTimedRunnable* as a regular functional interface with static rather than default methods that cannot be overridden.

So when does it make sense to use default methods and when does it make sense to use static methods? First, just as in regular interfaces, static methods are useful as helper methods that need not have access to state. Static methods must do their thing without needing to access instance methods in that object. Default methods, on the other hand, can access any method in the object. Second, static methods are not polymorphic. They cannot override their super interfaces and cannot shadow them. As a general rule, use default methods in functional interfaces whenever you would use instance methods in classes. Likewise, use static methods whenever you would use them instead of instance methods in classes.

Static methods further limit access to state because they cannot operate on the lambda instance that incarnates them. They are very much aligned to the functional virtue of limiting state.

Wrap up

This completes our tour of new syntactical additions to Java 8. But there is still some lambda fine print to consider. We look at that next.

Key points

● Java 8 introduces functional interfaces upon which lambdas are backed.

● Functional interfaces must declare exactly one non-default, non-static method. This is the single abstract method (or SAM) rule.

● The new *@FunctionalInterface* annotation can be used to ensure interfaces comply with the SAM rule at compile time. This annotation is optional but lambdas must still be backed by interfaces that respect the SAM rule, whether annotated or not.

● Method references can replace lambdas whenever lambdas do nothing more than act as bridges to other methods.

● Method references can be of the static, instance, super, constructor, generic constructor, and array constructor kind.

● Anonymous implementations still have their place in Java when classes are designed in an object-oriented style. Otherwise, lambdas should be used.

● Interfaces can contain method implementations when denoted with the *default* keyword. Default methods can provide behavior that can be overridden by a concrete class.

● Default methods can be instance or static based.

● Default methods introduce the possibility of class hierarchies defining the same methods across different lineages (also known as the diamond problem). Java 8 defines rules to resolve ambiguity and syntax to explicitly choose behavior.

Chapter 4: The fine print

So far, we've explored the broad strokes. We'll complete the anatomy of the lambda by examining the finer details. We'll look at the lexical scoping rules and round out the discussing with odd and ends.

Lexical scoping rules

Throughout this part, we've been comparing anonymous classes and lambdas. This will help us understand how lexical scoping rules work with lambdas when compared to anonymous classes. When a lambda is created from within a method, it inherits its surrounding context. This is why the term closure is sometimes used interchangeably with lambda because its surrounding context is *enclosed* within the lambda. Lambdas have access to class attributes, method parameters, and local variables from their surroundings, just like anonymous classes, but accessibility varies.

Action	Lambda	Anonymous
Read/write access to enclosing class attributes	Yes	Yes
Read access to enclosing local variables	Yes	Yes
Write access to enclosing local variables	No	No
Shadowing local variables	No	Yes
Mutating state of local or class attributes	Yes	Yes

Table 1: Lexical scoping lambdas vs. anonymous classes

This table shows how lambdas and anonymous classes compare with respect to accessing state. To examine these closer, we create this functional interface used in the examples below:

```
@FunctionalInterface
public interface LambdaExecutor {
    public void execute(Object object);
}
```

Read/write access to enclosing class attributes

This first point refers to accessibility of class attributes in the surrounding class. Like anonymous classes, lambdas can read and write class attributes. In this example, *attribute* is not only accessible from within the lambda but can also be modified:

```
public class LexicalScoping {
    private Object attribute;

    public void readWriteClassAttributes() throws Exception {
        // attribute is a class attribute that can be read and
        // written inside of lambdas
        LambdaExecutor executor =
            (anInteger) -> attribute = anInteger;
        executor.execute(1);
        System.out.println(attribute); // prints 1
    }
}
```

After the execution of *readWriteClassAttributes()*, *attribute* will contain an *Integer* type with a value of 1. This goes against the grain of functional programming, which discourages or prohibits mutating class attributes and provoking side effects. It is nevertheless legal Java code. This is a gentle reminder of the compromises made between preserving legacy Java versus adherence to functional principles. Lambdas and anonymous classes are subject to the same rule.

Read access to enclosing local variable

Local variables are slightly trickier. Both anonymous classes and lambdas can read local variables defined within the method (including method parameters). However, until

Java 8, local variables had to be declared as *final* to ensure that anonymous classes did not mutate the value of the local variable. Java 8 waters down this restriction by introducing the notion of *effectively final*. While local variables still only have read-only rights, they need not be explicitly declared as final. A non-final local variable read from a lambda is said to be *effectively final*. That is, even though the variable is non-final, it is final in principle if not in name. Mutation will be forbidden.

```java
public void readLocalVariable() {
    // No need to declare localAttribute as final in Java 8
    Object localAttribute = 1;

    // Accessing a local attribute within a lambda is permitted
    LambdaExecutor executor =  anObject ->
        System.out.println("Accessing localAttribute: " +
                            localAttribute);
    executor.execute(null);
}
```

Even though *localAttribute* is not final, it is permitted to access *localAttribute* from the lambda because it doesn't change its value. Lambdas and anonymous classes are subject to the same rules.

Write access to enclosing local variable

As with anonymous classes, lambdas cannot mutate local variables of the enclosing method. The following code snippet still fails to compile because mutation is attempted on *localAttribute*:

```java
public void writeLocalVariable() {
    Object localAttribute;

    // Illegal: cannot modify a local attribute from within a
    // lambda
    LambdaExecutor executor = anInt -> localAttribute = anInt;
    executor.execute(1);
}
```

As always, the compiler still forbids writing to local variables just as it does with anonymous classes. Be careful, though, with some hidden subtleties of effectively final.

Once the local variable is tagged as effectively final, you cannot modify its value even within the enclosing method:

```java
public void writeEffectivelyFinal() {
    Object localAttribute = 1;

    // localAttribute will now lose its effectively final status and
    // will no longer be allowed within the lambda.
    localAttribute = 2;
    LambdaExecutor executor =
        anInteger ->
            System.out.println("Accessing localAttribute: " +
                                    localAttribute);   // Fails compilation
    executor.execute(null);
}
```

The variable *localVariable* was allowed to be used within the lambda until the compiler noticed its value was changed to 2. Effectively final applies not only to the lambda but to the enclosing method as well.

Why is it illegal for a lambda to use non-final local variables? Anonymous classes have always had this restriction and it continues with Java 8. However, lambdas make an even stronger case for it. First, it is possible to capture a local variable within a lambda that only gets executed at a later point. Imagine if this code were legal:

```java
public LambdaExecutor getLambdaExecutor() {
    Object localAttribute = 1;

    // Not legal because localAttribute cannot be modified
    return anObject -> localAttribute = 2;
}
```

The lambda returned by *getLambdaExecutor()* would outlive the local variable *localAttribute*. This would pose a problem because local variables are destroyed when they go out of scope. So the Java platform could not support keeping *localAttribute* alive as long as the *lambdaExecutor* lambda. Second, lambdas work hand in hand with some of the standard libraries (discussed in part III) and those are meant to be used in parallel context with multiple threads. Having a mutable local variable shared amongst different threads would introduce new data race problems. There is no support in the Java platform for multi-threaded write access to local variables. Finally, state mutation and parallel processing is an incompatible mix with the functional programming mindset. The bottom line is that lambdas, like anonymous classes, require final local variables but at least the compiler can now infer finality and no longer needs the *final* keyword.

Shadowing local variables

Shadowing of variables is one area where anonymous classes differ from lambdas. With the former, it is permitted to re-declare a variable local to the anonymous class if it already exists in the enclosing method. This is known as *shadowing.* This next example shows how *localAttribute*, a local variable, is redefined as a local variable in the lambda:

```
public void shadowLocalVariables() {
    Object localAttribute;

    // The lambda parameter localAttribute is shadowing the local
    // variable localAttribute and prohibited by the compiler
    LambdaExecutor executor = localAttribute -> localAttribute = 1;
    executor.execute(1);
}
```

Shadowing of local variables is not allowed in lambdas but perfectly legal for anonymous classes:

```
public void shadowLocalVariablesAnonymous() {
    Object localAttribute;

    LambdaExecutor executor = new LambdaExecutor() {
        // localAttribute shadowing is legal for anonymous classes
        @Override
        public void execute(Object localAttribute) {
            // Do something
        }
    };

    executor.execute(1);
}
```

Mutating state of local or class attributes

This section would be incomplete without mentioning that Java offers no automatic mechanism to manage inner state mutation of class attributes. The next code snippet shows that *attribute* is being mutated with the *append()* call. Lambdas, as anonymous classes or final declarations, offer no way to forbid this.

```
public void mutatingState() {
    // Assign a StringBuffer to the class attribute named attribute
    attribute = new StringBuffer();

    // Inner state of attribute is mutated inside the lambda
    LambdaExecutor executor =
        aString -> ((StringBuffer) attribute).append(aString);
    executor.execute("another string");
}
```

Here, *attribute* is modified from inside the lambda.

Lambda leftovers

Throughout part II, we've talked about lambdas in fair detail. We've seen how lambdas can address Java's verbosity problem and how intent can be expressed succinctly. Even if you want to opt-out of functional programming, lambdas are a great tool even if only as a replacement for anonymous classes. There's a lot more to functional programming than lambdas, which we'll discuss in later chapters. We conclude this section with some lambda fine print.

By now, it should be clear that lambdas work with interfaces only. They conform to a specific functional interface, which can be denoted with the *@FunctionalInterface* annotation, and are manipulated via this handle. Also, lambdas are stateless. Recalling one of the major points introduced in the first chapter, there is no state in functional programming. More specifically, though, there is no conversational state. Since lambdas conform to functional interfaces, there cannot be any class attributes associated to the instance. State can only exist within method parameters, local variables, or public static variables. They are kept for the duration of the method call and returned or destroyed at the end.

Lambdas are also single-use constructs. When you define a lambda within a block of code and invoke its method, a new instance is created. When that instance is no longer reachable via its reference, it is garbage collected—just like any other object. Executing that block of code again will repeat the creation/invocation/destruction process. There is no lambda object pooling and no caching done by the runtime. You can, however, re-invoke a lambda method multiple times and this will invoke the same instance.

Although they themselves cannot be extended, lambdas implicitly extend from the *Object* super type and expose all public *Object* methods—just like regular objects. This means, for example, that they expose the usual *getClass(), hashCode(), equals()*, and *toString()* inherited from *Object*. Lambdas cannot actually implement these methods, because they can only implement one method, but the Java compiler supplies a default implementation similar to any other class extending *Object*. One peculiarity is the *getClass().getName()* method, which will return a string conforming to this template:

HolderClass$$Lambda$n

Where:

- **HolderClass**: Is the name of the class in which the lambda was defined.
- **Lambda**: Is a constant denoting that this is a lambda.
- **n**: Is the lambda creation count. Iterating through a block of code that creates a lambda would increment the *n* value by one during every loop.

Once instantiated, lambdas co-exist amongst other objects and behave just like regular objects. In fact, they *are* regular objects. They are handled via their functional interface and are indistinguishable from other objects.

Lambdas cannot be declared and invoked at once; they must first be assigned to a variable (or method parameter or class attribute) before being used. While it is perfectly legal to create an object and invoke a method:

```
String string = "Hello".append("There");
```

Applying the same thinking to lambdas would produce illegal Java code:

```
@FunctionalInterface
public interface StringExecutor {
    public String execute(String string);
}

// Certainly not legal!
(StringExecutor executor = s -> s + "There").execute("Hello");
```

Lambdas can throw exceptions just like anonymous classes. They can throw unchecked exceptions but must conform to their backing functional interface if they throw checked exceptions. The usual rules apply. Functional interfaces can also be generic and very often are. This is a double-edged sword because having generic functional interfaces means they can be used for any type. However, they also make lambdas more difficult to parse for developers. Not only must the developer get used to lambdas as code containers rather than code to execute immediately, but wrapping them in generics doubles the effort required to parse them. Practice makes perfect!

Our first lambda examples used the full syntax for parameter declaration:

(Type parameter, ...) -> Lambda block/expression or method reference

All of our subsequent examples followed the compact form:

parameters -> Lambda block/expression or method reference

The question arises: when is the full parameter syntax useful? You only need parentheses if multiple arguments are declared in the lambda. Otherwise, the reality is that you will rarely need to use the long form where parameter types are declared. In most cases, the compiler will automatically determine the lambda's parameter type. However, there are rare cases when methods employ generic functional interfaces as parameters and these sometimes require the developer to help the compiler determine the type. In such cases, the lambda parameter types must be declared.

As for lambda bodies, lambda expressions allow you to do away with braces, semi-colons, and return keywords. Otherwise, you must revert to lambda blocks. The compiler imposes no restriction on the size of a lambda block but having long blocks goes against what the language designers had in mind. Functional programming and conciseness are very good friends and go hand-in-hand. If you find yourself writing long blocks, consider splitting your code into smaller pieces and/or using method references. Long blocks go against the grain of functional programming.

Lambda byte code

Java 7 introduced the new byte code instruction *invoke dynamic* as part of JSR-292. This instruction was originally intended to be used solely by other JVM languages. Java 8 starts using this byte code natively for lambdas. *Invoke dynamic* allows method calls to be bound to their destination at runtime—contrary to *static invoke,* which binds the two at compilation time. Until now, the Java compiler has generated the *static invoke* byte code for all method invocations. With Java 8, compiling a lambda call generates the *invoke dynamic* byte code. When you consider that anonymous classes generate their own class files upon compilation (lambdas do not), and that byte code generated from lambdas is slightly more concise, functional programming is more concise not only in source code but byte code too!

Wrap up

We have now exposed all matters related to the lambda. We continue our tour of Java 8 with a look at the new libraries.

Key points

- Anonymous classes and lambdas are similar with respect to lexical scoping. The only difference is with respect to shadowing local variables. Anonymous classes allow shadowing while lambdas do not.

- Java 8 introduces the concept of effectively final. Local attributes used in lambdas and anonymous classes need not be declared as final as long as their values are not modified.

- Once instantiated, lambdas are regular objects and indistinguishable from other objects. They are garbage collected like any other object.

- Lambdas inherit from the super *Object* type like any object. Lambdas can be generic and throw exceptions just like any other object.

- Lambdas generate their own byte code. They use *invoke dynamic*, the new byte code instruction introduced in Java 7.

PART III
Java's Functional Trinity:
Functions, Collections & Streams

In part II, we laid the foundation of functional programming concepts. We are now going to build upon this and explore the functional libraries in Java. If lambdas are words in functional programming, Java 8's functional libraries are sentences where complete thoughts are formed.

Many newer programming languages have been conceived with functional programming in mind. This is normal as language designers (and developers using them) have come to realize that the functional philosophy is well suited to solve modern day programming problems. But they've had the luxury of designing functional programming from the ground up. Java has a legacy to consider and has instead opted to functionalize the language *at the library level*. As we've seen in part II, the syntax has been minimally changed to accommodate functional programming and limited to only three new symbols:

- ->
- ::
- default

Thus its newly found functional flavor has been baked into the new functional libraries rather than in the syntax. Java's language designers deliberately chose this path. Syntax changes tend to be more disruptive to programming languages and Java has always had a conservative slant. Not all Java developers will accept the functional philosophy and many will opt out. Developers are expected to know the entirety of a language's syntax but not necessarily the mastery of all its libraries—especially not in Java's library-rich ecosystem. Having functional programming realized at the library modularizes the paradigm.

On the flip side, expressing functional code in libraries is treating functional programming as a second-class citizen. As a non-native concept, functional programming will feel slightly less natural, be slightly more verbose, and require more patience to learn. It's a balancing act between respecting Java's past and adopting new ideas, especially in a language with a huge industry footprint.

In part II, we saw how Java carefully introduced the lambda into the language. Part III will show how Java realizes its full functional programming potential. This can be seen as the functional trinity that includes these Java packages:

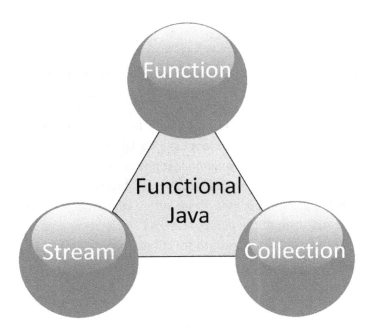

Figure 5: Java's key functional libraries

They are:

- **Function**: Chapter 3 discussed functional interfaces and how they back lambdas. It also briefly touched upon the standard functional interfaces, which are defined in the new *Functions* package. These interfaces are used throughout the Java standard libraries and can also be used for your own classes for everyday functional programming. We explore the *Function* package in chapter 5.
- **Collection**: The Collections library has been refreshed and functionalized. The *Map*, *List*, and *Set* interfaces have been revamped to enable and facilitate functional programming. Changes have been made at the top level of the class hierarchy and affect all subclasses and interfaces. We'll demonstrate how to use them.
- **Stream**: The *Stream* package is the most exciting addition to Java 8 and showcases functional programming at its best. Streams allow entire algorithms to be expressed in a declarative form. We'll dive deep into streams in chapters 7 and 8 and show how imperative algorithms can be ported to streams.

Be warned that learning to use these new features will not be like learning to use a new API or framework; it will be like learning a brand new way of thinking! If you are new to functional programming, expect the transition to be rough at times. If you are transitioning from other functional languages, you will have to adapt to Java's unique adaptation of functional programming.

Let's begin!

Chapter 5:
Functions & collections

Functional interfaces

As we saw in part II, lambdas must always be backed by a functional interface. This was a deliberate language design choice allowing lambdas to look just like any other object once created. However, it would be inconvenient to have to create a new functional interface every time we need to express a lambda. To overcome this inconvenience, the JDK ships with a package named *java.util.function* that contains 40-something functional interfaces. Typical lambdas you'll create everyday will easily conform to one of these. Unless you need very particular method signatures, you'll never need to create your own.

While 40 may seem like a formidable package to master, they really boil down to four usage patterns or what can be described (by this author) as four families of functional interfaces.

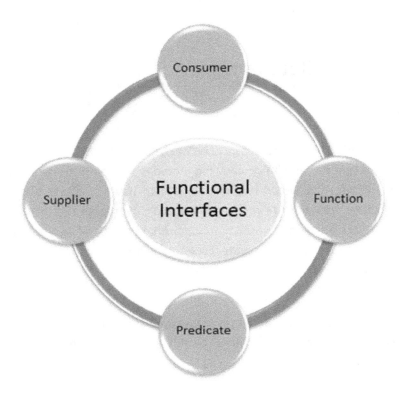

Figure 6: The four families of functional interfaces

It is more important to focus on the families of interfaces rather than each individual one. Besides, once the families are understood, it is intuitive to reach out for the right interface within a family. Each has one archetype interface and a handful of specialized variants to facilitate interaction with primitives or to vary function arity (the number of parameters used in a method). For example, the *Consumer* family is represented by the *Consumer* archetype interface. It also includes a handful of variants such as *DoubleConsumer*, *IntConsumer*, *LongConsumer*, and *BiConsumer*. As you would expect, *DoubleConsumer* is a specialization of *Consumer* that deals in *double* primitives, as are *int* and *long* to their respective interfaces. On the other hand, *BiConsumer* is a variation on arity; it is a two-type generic interface accepting two parameters instead of one.

These functional interfaces are frequently generic, allowing maximum applicability. They are also used by other JDK libraries, and you can expect them to be used by 3rd parties as well.

Let's take a look at each family of functional interfaces.

The Consumer functional interface family

We begin with the simplest of all: the *Consumer* family of functional interfaces.

Archetype
```
@FunctionalInterface
public interface Consumer<T> {
    void accept(T t);
}
```

Abstract Consume and discard

Variants
BiConsumer<T, U>	*ObjDoubleConsumer<T>*
DoubleConsumer	*ObjIntConsumer<T>*
IntConsumer	*ObjLongConsumer<T>*
LongConsumer	

The *Consumer* interface has a consume and discard semantic in which the sending and receiving parties are detached from one another. Since the *accept()* method does not return a value, it cannot communicate a result back to the caller. Thus the caller is not impacted by the behavior defined in the *Consumer* (unless the contents of object *T* are mutated—something the Java language does not prevent). The *Consumer* is useful in cases where processing is intercepted to inspect state or to perform any kind of work orthogonal to the caller.

The method *computeShapeArea()* shown below computes the area of a shape with a given number of angles and dimensions:

```java
public static double computeShapeArea
    (int angles, double measure1, double measure2,
     Consumer<String> consumer) {
    double area;
    switch (angles) {
        case 0 : {
            // Circle: measure1 is radius
            area = Math.PI * Math.pow(measure1, 2);
            consumer.accept("Area formula for shape with " + angles +
                            " angles is pi times radius: " + Math.PI +
                            " times " + measure1 + " squared = " +
                            area);
            break;
        }

        case 3 : {
            // Triangle: measure1 is base, measure2 is height
            area = measure1 * measure2 / 2;
            consumer.accept("Area formula for shape with " + angles +
                            " angles is height times base divided by"
                            + " 2: " + measure1 + " times " +
                            measure2 + " divided by 2 = " + area);
            break;
        }

        case 4 : {
            // Rectangle or square: measure1 is width, measure2 is
            // length
            area = measure1 * measure2;
            consumer.accept("Area formula for shape with " + angles +
                            " angles is width times length: " +
                            measure1 + " times " + measure2 + " = " +
                            area);
            break;
        }

        default: {
            throw new RuntimeException("Unsupported shape with " +
                                    angles + " angles");
        }
    }

    return area;
}
```

The method *computeShapeArea()* will use a different calculation depending on the number of angles. The caller would like to know which formula was used for the calculation. This is done via the *Consumer* interface. This gives the caller the opportunity to do what it wishes with that information. For example:

```
// Caller code
computeShapeArea(0, 7, 0, System.out::println);   // Circle
computeShapeArea(3, 8, 2, System.out::println);   // Triangle
computeShapeArea(4, 10, 5, System.out::println); // Rectangle

// Prints
// Area formula for shape with 0 angles is pi times radius:
// 3.141592653589793 times 7.0 squared = 153.93804002589985
// Area formula for shape with 3 angles is height times base divided
// by 2: 8.0 times 2.0 divided by 2 = 8.0
// Area formula for shape with 4 angles is width times length: 10.0
// times 5.0 = 50.0
```

Here, the caller defines a lambda with a *println()* method reference. The *computeShapeArea()* method is completely detached from the *println()*.

The Function functional interface family

Archetype
```
public interface Function<T, R> {
    R apply(T t);
}
```

Abstract Map, transform, compute

Variants

BiFunction<T, U, R>	*ToDoubleFunction<T>*
BinaryOperator<T>	*ToIntBiFunction<T, U>*
DoubleFunction<R>	*ToIntFunction<T>*
DoubleToIntFunction	*ToLongBiFunction<T, U>*
DoubleToLongFunction	*ToLongFunction<T>*
IntFunction<R>	*DoubleBinaryOperator*
IntToDoubleFunction	*DoubleUnaryOperator*
IntToLongFunction	*IntBinaryOperator*
LongFunction<R>	*IntUnaryOperator*
LongToDoubleFunction	*LongBinaryOperator*
LongToIntFunction	*LongUnaryOperator*
ToDoubleBiFunction<T, U>	*UnaryOperator<T>*

The *Function* family of functional interfaces transforms one value to another of the same or different kind. It fits the input-process-output mold compatible with methods that perform calculations. As a generic type, it allows the type of *T* and *R* to be specified. There are many variants that offer type specializations. Notice also that some variants have the *operator* suffix. These sometimes extend the *Function* interface, such as *UnaryOperator*, and specialize the generic types. Others, such as the *IntUnaryOperator*, simply offer a non-generic variant. In this example, *IntUnaryOperator* is a non-generic variant of *IntFunction*. While few have a parent/child interface relationship, they are related by their common semantics.

Continuing with our previous example of area computation, we refactor the example to let the caller specify which formula to use:

```
public static double computeShapeArea
    (double measure1, double measure2,
     BiFunction<Double, Double, Double> function) {
    return function.apply(measure1, measure2);
}
```

This is achieved via the *BiFunction* interface, which is a two-parameter variant of *Function*. We could also have used *DoubleBinaryOperator* as a non-generic alternative. Now, *computeShareArea()* is a bare-boned method because all it needs to do is pass the parameters to the method, which will calculate the area.

The caller code looks like this:

```
// Area formula for a rectangle (returns 50.0)
computeShapeArea(10, 5, (w, l) -> w * l);
```

While *computeShapeArea()* is not terribly useful as a one-liner method, this example demonstrates that *Function* is a very useful container for behavior injection. It has a wide range of applicability and you will be reaching out for this interface as a backbone to many of your lambdas.

The Predicate functional interface family

Archetype
```
public interface Predicate<T> {
        boolean test(T t);
    }
```

Abstract Test, Filter

Variants *BiPredicate<T, U>*   *IntPredicate*
              DoublePredicate   *LongPredicate*

The *Predicate* family defines the semantics for test conditions and is often used for filtering data. There are only four variants offering type specialization. One of them, *BiPredicate*, offers arity variation with two parameters instead of one.

We can enrich our area calculator with a *BiPredicate,* which lets the caller determine whether computations should be rounded based on an arbitrary condition. For example:

```
public static double computeShapeArea
    (double measure1, double measure2, DoubleBinaryOperator function,
      BiPredicate<Double, Double> roundUpPredicate) {
    double area = function.applyAsDouble(measure1, measure2);
    // Let the predicate decide whether or not to round the
    // calculation
    return roundUpPredicate.test(measure1, measure2) ?
          Math.rint(area) : area;
}
```

And the caller code:

```
// Round off calculation of area if either w or l is > 100
// (returns 22.0)
computeShapeArea
    (5.5, 4, (w, l) -> w * l,  (w, l) -> w > 100 || l > 100);
```

Here, we supply the *Predicate* which returns true if either *measure1* or *measure2* is greater than 100. This will result in the area calculation being rounded off for big areas.

The *Predicate* family also has a wide range of applicability—especially within the Streams library.

The Supplier functional interface family

Archetype
```
public interface Supplier<T> {
    T get();
}
```

Abstract Create

Variants
BooleanSupplier   *IntSupplier*
DoubleSupplier   *LongSupplier*

The final family is the *Supplier* interface. It is designed for lambdas that must supply objects through creation or other means. The variants, as usual, simply offer type specializations.

Completing our area calculator example, we can use a *Supplier* to create the parameters used in the formula:

```
public static double computeShapeArea
    (Supplier<Double> measure1, Supplier<Double> measure2,
     DoubleBinaryOperator function) {
    // Determine measure1 and measure2 from Supplier
    return function.applyAsDouble(measure1.get(), measure2.get());
}
```

And the caller code now supplies lambdas for parameters instead of actual values:

```
// Pass 5.0 and 5.1 via the supplier interface and calculate
// the area of a
// triangle (return 12.75).
computeShapeArea(() -> 5.0, () -> 5.1, (h, b) -> h * b / 2);
```

Now, the values are computed via the *Supplier* interface.

Suppliers can be used as a replacement for factory Design Patterns, which generate objects. In fact, they are their functional programming equivalent. We'll discuss this in greater detail in chapter 8.

Other functional interfaces

In addition to the new standard functional interfaces, an old interface has been revamped for Java 8. The *Comparator* interface is now a functional interface marked with the *@FunctionalInterface* annotation. The semantically-related *Comparable* interface, however, is still not. Both the *Comparable* and *Comparator* interfaces are used to compare objects for semantic equivalence and have existed in Java since version 1.2. However, *Comparable* is an object-oriented way of performing comparison whereas *Comparator* is a functionally styled one. *Comparable* defines one method, *compareTo(T o)*, and compares the given value with its own stored as state. On the other hand, *Comparator*, with its method *compare(T o1, T, o2)*, expects both values to be supplied by the caller. Lambdas are incompatible with *Comparable* because they cannot hold state. *Comparator* is a lambda-friendly alternative and a logical choice to be a functional interface. It also defines a slew of default and static methods to facilitate functional composition—a topic we discuss next.

The standard functional interfaces go a long way in giving what you need as the backbone to all your custom lambdas. For the detailed list of Java 8 functional interfaces, see the appendix.

Functional composition

The standard functional interfaces deal in the currency of behavior. They are vehicles that ease the creation and exchange of behavior and are designed specifically for lambdas. With this purpose in mind, the standard functional interfaces explored in this chapter are packaged with a set of default methods enabling an important aspect of functional programming: functional composition. Functional composition is a technique used in functional programming that combines two or more independent functions to form a brand new super function. It's a Lego approach to programming.

Recall that when functional interfaces are incarnated, they become regular objects but are behavior-centric and contain only the lambda to be executed as their state (via *invoke dynamic*). These default methods access the embedded lambda to re-order and re-compose behavior.

Let's see how this works starting with the *Consumer* interface.

Consumer composition

The *Consumer* interface defines the *andThen()* default method:

```
default Consumer<T> andThen(Consumer<? super T> after) {
    return (T t) -> { accept(t); after.accept(t); };
}
```

This is one representation of the concept of higher-order functions in action—the idea of a function returning another function. The method *andThen()* builds a brand new *Consumer* by aggregating itself and the function contained in *after*. It now gives the caller a brand new super function that performs that action contained in this instance of *Consumer and then* calls the function contained in *after*. From the caller's point of view, it's a *Consumer* like any other and that's the beauty. Let's start off with a simple example to illustrate the point.

In this example, we define two standalone functions:

- Print the given value to the console
- Print the given value to the logging system

These two functions work independently of each other yet can be combined to work together as one. We define *printToOut* to print to the standard out and *printToLog* to log by message severity:

```
Logger logger = Logger.getLogger("ConsumerLogger");
Consumer<String> printToOut = System.out::println;
Consumer<String> printToLog =
    s -> {
            // Log the message as severe if it contains the word
            // "critical"
            if (s.contains("critical")) {
                logger.severe(s);
            }
            else {
                logger.info(s);
            };
        }
```

Now let's use *andThen()* to fuse the two and create a new super function.

```
Consumer<String> superPrinter = printToOut.andThen(printToLog);
```

This line is executed exactly as it is read. First, print the value to the standard out, *and then* print to the logging system. We can execute the *Consumer* like this:

```
superPrinter.accept("Hello"); // Prints to out and log as INFO
superPrinter.accept("This is critical"); // Print to out and log
                                         // as SEVERE
```

Composition is a powerful concept. It unlocks a new way to think about code modularity. It allows unrelated commands to be composed and used in unforeseen ways. There are no limits to the amount of *Consumers* that can be chained together. For example:

```
Consumer<String> superPrinter =
    // Consumers can be chained endlessly
    printToOut.andThen(printToLog).andThen(…);
```

Consumer is just one of the many functional interfaces that have built-in composition such as *andThen()*. Most variants of the *Consumer* family also offer *andThen()* composition. We look at *Predicate* next.

Predicate composition

Recall that the *Predicate* interface deals in logical operations. Its abstract method is *test()*, which returns a boolean response. *Predicate* is armed with three default methods that permit logical conditions to be constructed from two functions. They are:

```
default Predicate<T> and(Predicate<? super T> other) {
        return (t) -> test(t) && other.test(t);
}

default Predicate<T> or(Predicate<? super T> other) {
        return (t) -> test(t) || other.test(t);
}

default Predicate<T> negate() {
        return (t) -> !test(t);
}
```

The *and()* and *or()* simply combine the given predicate with themselves and return a new predicate. The negate returns the opposite of itself in the *test()* method. We can use these methods in interesting ways.

We can use *IntPredicate*, the integer specialization of *Predicate*, to illustrate this next example. Suppose that we define a predicate that determines whether or not the given integer is indivisible.

```
IntPredicate isIndivisible = i -> {
            for (int n = 2; n <= Math.sqrt(i); ++n)
                if (i % n == 0)
                    return false;

            return true;
    };
```

This predicate *isIndivisible* defines a lambda that determines whether the integer *i* is divisible or not. It could also be used as a lambda that determines primarity (whether or not a number is prime), except that it would have a flaw. When tested against the value 1, it would return true. However, 1 is not a prime number. Rather than break *isIndivisible()*, let's use composition.

First, we create a brand new *IntPredicate*:

```
IntPredicate isGreaterThanOne = i -> i > 1;
```

And now we use composition to create a new *Predicate* out of the two to test for primarity:

```
IntPredicate isPrime = isGreaterThanOne.and(isIndivisible);
isPrime.test(1); // Returns false-1 is not a prime number
```

Again, the line reads like a sentence: A number is prime if it is greater than one *and* is indivisible. The normal short-circuiting feature of Java *if* statements takes effect in the *and* statement. That is, if a number is one, the test for indivisibility will not be executed.

What if we wanted a function to test if a number is a composite[3]? We can't just negate the *isPrime* because testing for the value of 1 would again yield an incorrect answer. We could do this instead:

```
IntPredicate isComposite=
isIndivisible.negate().and(isGreaterThanOne);
isComposite.test(1); // Returns false-1 is not a composite number
                     // either
```

These basic examples show that logical composition works its magic when we create functions that are atomic and do only one thing. In this example, we had two functions that only did one thing but were combined to form the condition required to test for a prime number. It's a simple concept that takes a little time to appreciate.

Function composition

We conclude our discussion on composition by looking at what the *Function* family of interfaces has to offer. Recall that *Function*'s abstract method is *apply()*, which receives a parameter and returns another. This is well suited for mapping or transformation functions that convert one value to another.

The *Function* interface defines two composition methods:

---

[3] A number greater than one that is not prime.

```
default <V> Function<V, R> compose
    (Function<? super V, ? extends T> before) {
    return (V v) -> apply(before.apply(v));
}

default <V> Function<T, V> andThen
    (Function<? super R, ? extends V> after) {
        return (T t) -> after.apply(apply(t));
}
```

A good parallel to draw from is the Linux/Unix operating system, which has proven the power of composition decades ago.

The Linux shell has a finite set of command-line operations. Each is atomic and only does one thing. However, their true power comes from the fact that they can be recombined in infinite ways to create new commands. For example, if we wanted to list all processes that run Java on the host, we can use two disparate Linux commands, *ps* and *grep*, and combine them with the Linux pipe feature: *ps –ef | grep java*.

Here's what this would look like in Java using *Function*'s *andThen()* methods:

```
Function<List<String>, List<String>> ps = … // details not important
Function<List<String>, List<String>> grep = …
                                        // details not important
Function<List<String>, List<String>> listJavaProcs = ps.andThen(grep);

// Pass null to apply because the ps lambda does not use its
// parameter
for (String nextProcess : listJavaProcs.apply(null)) {
    // Print the contents of the result
    System.out.println(nextProcess);
}
```

ListJavaProcs is a brand new function that fuses the two. Think of *andThen()* as Java's pipe equivalent. Just as you can pipe repeatedly in Linux, you can compose as many functions as you like by chaining them with *andThen()*. For example:

```
// Get the system processes, grep on "java", and count the lines
ps.andThen(grep).andThen(wcLines);
```

We've now defined a new function to count the number of Java processes.

A variation of the same theme is the *compose()* method. It works in reverse order of *andThen()*. It calls the given function first, then calls itself. Again, we can draw a parallel from Linux. If we wanted to edit a script named *myScripts.sh* not knowing where the file exists on the file system, but knowing that it is somewhere on the *$PATH*, we would use this:

```
Linux shell
$$> vi `which myScript.sh`
```

Here, the *which* command is first executed, then its output is given as the input to vi. Here's the Java equivalent:

```
Function<String, String> which = … // Details not important
Function<String, String> vi = … // Details not important

Function<String, String> viWhich = vi.compose(which);
```

Superficially, the only difference between *andThen()* and *compose()* is the order of execution: *andThen()* executes the function defined in itself first, then the given one. The *compose()* method works in reverse order. As such, you can achieve the same results using only *andThen()* and reversing the parameters.

```
// Equivalent to: viWhich = vi.compose(which);
Function<String, String> viWhich = which.andThen(vi);
```

However, there is a more subtle difference. *Function*'s generic types must be compatible. The *compose()* methods' input function must have an output compatible with the composed input parameter. With *andThen()*, it's the opposite: its function must output a value compatible with the input of the composed function. This is evident with the different signature of *compose()* and *andThen()*. Stated another way: *andThen()* reads left-to-right while *compose()* reads right-to-left.

This completes our overview of functional composition as offered by the functional interfaces. Functional composition is the entry point into more advanced concepts in functional programming. It makes you think about class design differently. We'll revisit this topic in chapter 8.

Functionalizing Collections

When we externalize code, we expose every step. This is the hallmark of imperative programming. However, one of the re-occurring themes of functional programming is the idea of doing the exact opposite: internalizing code. The act of internalizing code is to hide the details inside a function. But functional programming pushes this idea further by turning micro-patterns of everyday programming into functions. For example, iterating over data, be it with iterators, for-loops, or while-loops, is one of those micro-patterns. Functional programming changes the way we think about them.

Java's functionalization effort would not be complete without a revamp of its Collections library, namely the *Collection*, *Map*, *List* and *Set* interfaces. This is because iteration is often done over *collections* and they are the very fabric of Java programs. It is a natural place for the functionalization effort to occur. But making any kind of significant changes, like adding new methods to the *Collection* interface, would break backward compatibility to all programs written pre-Java 8. This includes not only the JDK's own hierarchy extending the *Collection* interface but any open or closed source 3rd party library and in-house classes. Java's designers have never and will never adopt such a strategy. Yet changes were necessary; the library was introduced in 1998, eons in software industry years, and was showing its age.

The motivation for the introduction of default methods was ushered by the need to modernize and functionalize the Collections library. Default methods are just the right tonic because they permit behavior to be added at the root of the hierarchy without disturbing dependent classes. Subclasses can either inherit or override the behavior. Unlike adding new interface methods, subclasses can automatically accept new default methods without recompilation. Instant compatibility is achieved. Default methods have proven useful in their own right but owe their existence to the need to functionalize the Collections library.

A second re-occurring theme in functional programming is parallelization. Quite simply, functional programming offers a better mousetrap for parallel processing. As a consequence, the Collections library has been enriched to benefit from multi-core CPUs when processing collections. Together with Streams (discussed later in this book), the

Collections library is at center stage in bringing functional-style parallel processing to Java.

Now that we've studied Java's standard functional interfaces, we can begin to apply that knowledge to Collections. Let's look at what has become of the Collections library in Java 8.

Collection interface

We start by looking at a brand new default method in the *Collection* interface available to lists and sets. This is the *forEach()* method:

```
// Defined in the Iterable interface and extended in Collection
default void forEach(Consumer<? super T> action)
```

This method iterates through the entire collection letting the *Consumer* decide what to do for each element. This is the concept of internal iteration and a manifestation of declarative programming. The details of how to iterate are not specified. This is in opposition to external iteration, where the details of how to iterate as well as what to do with each element are specified in code.

We will show examples of these functionalized collection methods with the slapstick comedy trio from the golden age of Hollywood films: Larry, Moe, and Curly of *The Three Stooges* fame. To start, let's print the contents of a collection:

```
Collection<String> stooges = Arrays.asList("Larry", "Moe", "Curly");
// Print the contents of the stooges collection
stooges.forEach(System.out::println);
```

The *forEach()* method has a very wide range of applicability. It is a much more convenient way to iterate through collections and should be your de-facto standard. However, being a declarative construct, there are some things you will not be able to do. You must abide by the rules of functional programming as described in chapter 1. Most notably, you cannot change the state of local variables like you could in a while-loop. Algorithms must be re-thought functionally. This is a more complex subject that will be discussed in chapter 8. For now, just know that *forEach()* is ideal for iterations that do not mutate state.

We now look at another new method available in *Collection*:

```
default boolean removeIf(Predicate<? super E> filter)
```

The method *removeIf()* internalizes the entire process of iterating, testing, and removing. It requires only to be told what the condition for removal is.

Using the now familiar *Predicate* functional interface, we can easily figure out what kind of lambda to use.

```
// Remove all people not part of The Three Stooges comedy trio
List<String> theThreeStooges = new ArrayList<>
    (Arrays.asList("Larry", "Moe", "Curly", "Tom", "Dick", "Harry"));

// Create the predicate that determines who is a stooge
Predicate<String> isAStooge =
    s -> "Larry".equals(s) || "Moe".equals(s) ||
        "Curly".equals(s);

// Negate the condition to remove non-stooges
theThreeStooges.removeIf(isAStooge.negate());
```

To replace all contents of a *List*, we can use *replaceAll()*:

```
List<String> theThreeStooges = new ArrayList<>
    (Arrays.asList("Larry", "Moe", "Curly"));

// Create the lambda to feminize the names
UnaryOperator<String> feminize =
    s -> "Larry".equals(s) ? "Lara" : "Moe".equals(s) ? "Maude" :
        "Shirley";

// Replace all male names with their female counterparts
theThreeStooges.replaceAll(feminize);
```

ReplaceAll() uses a *UnaryOperator* as its functional interface, which is a *Function* sub interface.

Both *replaceIf()* and *replaceAll()* are available to all subclasses with one caveat: the underlying class must support removal or an exception will be thrown.

These examples show the compactness of functional programming. Most of the work was done by the function with the lambda providing the details.

Map interface

One of the biggest irritants of using lists as values in maps is the constant need to check for the presence of the map before adding, updating, or removing an element. First, you must try to extract the list and create it if it is not found. For example, say we have a method that updates a movie database implemented as a map. The map's key is the year of the movie and its value is a list of movies for that year. Pre-Java 8, the code would look like this:

```java
private Map<Integer, List<String>> movieDatabase = new HashMap<>();

private void addMovie(Integer year, String title) {
    List<String> movies = movieDatabase.get(year);

    if (movies == null) {
        // Need to create the array list if it doesn't yet exist
        movies = new LinkedList<String>();
        movieDatabase.put(year, movies);
    }

    movies.add(title);
}
```

Java 8 offers a better alternative with these default methods:

```
default V compute
    (K key,
     BiFunction<? super K, ? super V, ? extends V> remappingFunction)

default V computeIfPresent
    (K key,
     BiFunction<? super K, ? super V, ? extends V> remappingFunction)

default V computeIfAbsent
    (K key,
     Function<? super K, ? extends V> mappingFunction)

default V getOrDefault(Object key, V defaultValue);

default V putIfAbsent(K key, V value);

default V merge
    (K key, V value,
     BiFunction<? super V, ? super V, ? extends V> remappingFunction)
```

Let's start with the compute methods. Each variant allows the map's value to be generated by the mapping function. For *computeIfPresent()* and *computeIfAbsent()*, mapping occurs conditionally. So with these methods, we can refactor the previous code example:

```
private Map<Integer, List<String>> movieDatabase = new HashMap<>();

private void addMovie(Integer year, String title) {
    movieDatabase.computeIfAbsent(year, k -> new LinkedList<>());
    movieDatabase.compute(year,
        (k, v) -> {
                        // K is the key of the map (the year)
                        // V is the value containing the list
                        // strings (titles)
                        v.add(title);
                        return v;
                   });
}
```

Notice that the creation of the list is handled by the *computeIfAbsent()* lambda. When it is time to add the movie to the list, via the *compute()* method, the *add()* will never throw a *NullPointerException* because the list is guaranteed to have been created.

In this case, using the *computeIfAbsent()* method is overkill and we would be better off with *putIfAbsent()*:

```
movieDatabase.putIfAbsent(year, new LinkedList<>());
```

This method is lambda-less and expects a value to be given—not calculated. This is still a functional style method even though no lambda was used. It proves the point that you can express code functionally without necessarily using lambdas.

If you still need to extract the data, you can use a more functional approach with the *getOrDefault()* method:

```
movieDatabase.getOrDefault(year, new LinkedList<>());
```

You can also use the *merge()* method as an alternative. It facilitates the checking of the existence of a list. In the example below, if the key (*year*) doesn't exist in the map, it puts the value (*titles*) in the map. If it does exist, it allows a *BiFunction* to decide what to do with the two lists:

```
private Map<Integer, List<String>> movieDatabase = new HashMap<>();

private void addMovies(Integer year, List<String> titles) {
    // Merge the contents of the current list at key=year with titles
    movieDatabase.merge(year, titles,
        (t1, t2) -> {
                    // Append titles to current list—only gets
                    // called if a value is stored at this key.
                    // Otherwise, titles is stored.
                    t1.addAll(t2);
                    return t1;
                });
}
```

And it can be used this way:

```
List<String> titles =
    new ArrayList<>(Arrays.asList("Meet the Baron",
                                  "Nertsery Rhymes"));

movieDatabase.merge(1933, titles,
                    // BiFunction to append t2 to t1
                    (t1, t2) -> {t1.addAll(t2); return t1;});
```

The *BiFunction* can also return *null*, which tells the merge to delete the key.

The takeaway is that we have removed the overhead code of checking for the existence of an element and can now focus on what really matters: defining *how* to create the list and *how* to add an element to the list.

The map interface has been enriched with other functional methods such as *forEach()*, *replace()*, and *replaceAll()* and uses the same principle of code internalization. Consult the appendix for the complete listing.

Spliterator

The Collections library is still subject to the same constraints regarding concurrent access. As always, you must choose the Collections library class that corresponds to your thread safety requirements. This is because the new methods shown above are just functional abstractions riding above the same underlying data structures. These methods are not particularly amenable to functional programming's take on parallel processing because they are still based on the notion of multiple threads mutating the collection and synchronizing access to the underlying data. However, there exists a new Java 8 abstraction that *is* compatible. It is designed to iterate over data in parallel. The idea is embodied by the *Spliterator* interface. The premise of this interface is to partition the data and hand off chunks to different threads. *Spliterators* can be obtained from the *Collection* interface, including sub interfaces *List* and *Set*.

Central to the *Spliterator* interface are these three methods:

```
Spliterator<T> trySplit();

default void forEachRemaining(Consumer<? super T> action) {…}

boolean tryAdvance(Consumer<? super T> action);
```

The method *trySplit()* partitions the underlying data in two. It creates a new *Spliterator* with half the data and keeps the other half in the original instance. Each can be given to a thread which, in turn, iterates over the partitioned data using *forEachRemaining()*. The method *tryAdvance()* is a one-at-a-time variant that returns the next element or *null* if the list has been exhausted.

Spliterators do not handle parallel processing themselves but provide the abstraction to do so. Here's the concept in action:

```java
public static boolean isMovieInList(String title, List<String>
movieList)
    throws InterruptedException {
    // Obtain a spliterator from the movie list
    Spliterator<String> s1 = movieList.spliterator();

    // Split the original list in half.
    // Now s1 and s2 each contains half the list.
    Spliterator<String> s2 = s1.trySplit();

    BooleanHolder booleanHolder = new BooleanHolder();
    if (s2 != null) {
        Consumer<String> finder =
            movie ->
                {if (movie.equals(title)) booleanHolder.isFound = true;};

        // Each thread searches the movie list in parallel
        Thread t1 = new Thread(() -> s1.forEachRemaining(finder));
        Thread t2 = new Thread(() -> s2.forEachRemaining(finder));

        t1.start();
        t2.start();
        t1.join();
        t2.join();
    }

    return booleanHolder.isFound;
}

private static class BooleanHolder {
    public boolean isFound = false;
}
```

Given a title and a list of movies, the method *isMovieInList()* parallelizes the search to determine if it is contained in the list. It sets the flag in *booleanHolder* to true if found. It obtains a *Spliterator* instance from the list, splits it in half, and hands off one half to each thread. The splitting process can be repeated if further threads are available.

Spliterators can be obtained from other *Collection* types as well as other libraries in the JDK. There are many implementations designed that deal with different characteristics, including finite/infinite, ordered/non-ordered, sorted/non-sorted, and mutable/immutable. They inherit the qualities of their underlying data structure.

Spliterators are a lower-level abstraction designed to give you more fined-grained control over parallelized iteration. However, the API lacks some of the refinements needed to implement functionally-friendly algorithms. In the above example, we needed to store the state in the *BooleanHolder* for the search. In the next chapter, we will discuss Streams, which are higher-level abstractions and offer a much richer API to implement fully-functional algorithms.

Wrap up

This completes our overview of the new and improved Java 8 Collections library as well as the standard functional interfaces. Just as there have been many changes in the standard JDK libraries to support functional concepts, expect major changes from 3rd party APIs. But the biggest change is yet to come...

Key points

● The new package *java.util.function* contains a set of functional interfaces. These are grouped into four families, each represented by their archetypes: *Consumer*, *Function*, *Predicate*, and *Supplier*.

● Each family of functional interfaces defines variants that specialize on types and arity.

● Functional interfaces also define methods that enable functional composition. Multiple disparate lambdas can be fused to form super functions that appear as one.

● The Collections library has been revamped and functionalized. This has been achieved using default methods at top levels of the hierarchy, thereby ensuring backward compatibility.

● The new functional methods in *Collection*, *list*, *set*, and *map* have been designed with internal iteration in mind. Behavioral parameters in the form of lambdas and method references are given to methods that iterate over collections and act upon each element.

● Internal iteration is a form of declarative programming that is fundamental to functional programming. It relieves the developer from having to describe the "how" to do it and focuses instead on the "what" to do.

● *Spliterators* are designed for parallel iteration over collections. Data is partitioned and each chunk is handed to different threads for parallel processing.

Chapter 6: Streams

So far, we've been laying the foundation for functional programming—Java style. Everything we've discussed has been leading up to the *pièce de résistance*: streams. This is where the rubber meets the road; where we put into practice everything we've learned so far about functional programming. If Java can be said to be a functional language, streams are where this happens.

Streams are functional animals. When we say functional programming favors immutability, minimizes or avoids state, and aims for functional purity, streams are the very embodiment of this philosophy. When we talk about declarative programming and binding functions together without necessarily specifying their contents, we're looking at you, streams. Finally, when we talk about organizing processing into parallel workflows each dedicated to a core and avoiding state, shared resources, and locks, we're shouting "streams!"

In the academic world of functional programming, the very abstract term "monad" is used to describe a structure whereby operations are bound together to form a pipeline. Each operation processes a long, possibly infinite, stream of data and passes along its output to the next operation. But that description is meaningless to a non-functional programmer. A better way to describe streams is to think of them as conveyor belts on an assembly line. Data passes through streams as widgets pass through conveyor belts.

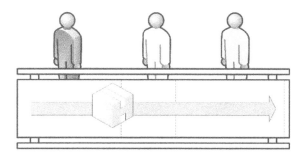

Figure 7: Streams as conveyor belts

Continuing with this analogy, each station is manned by a worker enriching the widget as it passes by. We can have any number of workers on the conveyor belt but care must be given because they must all be able to work cohesively as a whole. Each worker is a specialist that performs one type of job, and there are slight variations within each job description. There is also another aspect to their job descriptions: some are intermediates, working on widgets as they pass by, while others are terminal, finishing widgets at the end of the line. Just as it wouldn't make sense to put an intermediate worker at the end of the conveyor belt, it wouldn't make sense to put a terminal worker in the middle. Streams must be coherent.

Workers know how to get their jobs done but their work can be customized within their own job description. For example, a worker whose job is to inspect the contents to ensure they meet the standards can be told what those standards are. Once told about the criteria, however, the worker is responsible for executing. No need to intervene. An important quality of these workers is that they are lazy. If the box containing the widget did not meet the quality standards, there is no point in closing it. The box is discarded and taken off the conveyor belt. Some would say lazy is working smart.

We can use a general purpose conveyor belt to build any type of widget but sometimes it makes sense to use customized types for special kinds of widgets. The workers can then have more affinity towards the widget they are building.

What happens when production must be scaled up to meet increased demand? One easy way to do this is to speed up the conveyor belt (vertical scaling). But this solution achieves little because the workers can only speed up a little (workers are a bottleneck). The second solution is to double the workers at each post (multi-threading). But this too achieves little because now workers must be careful not to step on each other's toes. More frustratingly, though, is that one out of every 1000 widgets is built with defects and no one understands why; the workers seem to build perfect widgets when they practice (QA environment). These conditions only seem to exist on the real conveyor belt (production environment).

Suddenly, someone with a background in functional programming has an idea: why don't we put the extra workers on their own separate conveyor belts? Will this work? So long as the workers are truly interchangeable, it will work. They must not keep a memory of things (hold state), like keeping a count of widgets as they pass by, and must be able to process widgets identically, whether it's the first or one millionth (be functionally pure). While they modify the widget as it passes by, what they do to the widget (their behavior) is not affected by the time of day, the number of widgets that have passed by, or whether or not their favorite colleague is working next to them. With this, we can buy as many conveyor belts and hire as many workers as needed to scale out production.

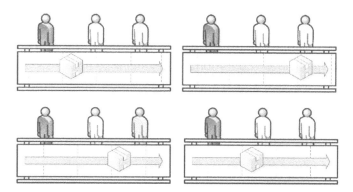

Figure 8: Scaling out production

What's interesting about this conveyor belt is that we don't need to specify how many are needed. Once we decide we want multiple conveyor belts, they automatically calibrate themselves to the amount needed. This gives us tremendous flexibility. This type of parallelism is much easier to program. If the workers work well on one conveyor belt, they will work just as well on ten conveyor belts, provided they obey the functional principles.

We can now relate this analogy back to streams. The conveyor belt is, of course, the stream itself. The workers are stream methods called *operations*. Their actions can be customized with *behavioral parameters* and expressed through lambdas or method references. The process used to build the widget is the algorithm. We can define entire algorithms traditionally used in imperative program in a series of stream operations that form pipelines.

Specialized streams can be used in lieu of generic ones to handle primitive types in the same way we saw functional interfaces specialized for primitive types. Finally, streams are powered by the fork-join framework when used to process in parallel. Let's dig deeper, starting with stream operations.

Stream operations

Streams are part of the new package named *java.util.stream*. They are just a set of interfaces with abstract, default, and static methods. In the context of streams, these methods are known as operations. There are many different types of operations, but this author likes to think about operations as belonging to one of six distinct families:

Figure 9: The six families of stream operations

Operations allow entire algorithms to be expressed declaratively. Typical algorithms iterate over sets of data, filtering some data out, keeping some other data in, transforming and computing values, and possibly reducing entire data sets to single values. All of these actions can be done by stream operations.

Operations are rooted in functional programming theory. You will find conceptually similar constructs in other functional languages. However, they will likely be embedded within the language's own syntax. Streams are an example of how Java has realized functional programming at the library level instead.

Let's take a look at these operations, family by family.

For the tables below, operations implemented as static methods are marked *stat* whereas instance-based operations are marked *inst*. Each includes their continuity (*inter* for intermediate or *term* for terminal). Consult the appendix for full method signatures of stream operations.

Build operations

Abstract   Create and start the stream process

Operations

concat(Stream<? extends T> a, Stream<? extends T> b)	*Inter*	*Stat*
empty()	*Inter*	*Stat*
generate(Supplier<T> s)	*Inter*	*Stat*
iterate(final T seed, final UnaryOperator<T> f)	*Inter*	*Stat*
of(T t)	*Inter*	*Stat*
of(T... values)	*Inter*	*Stat*
onClose(Runnable closeHandler)	*Inter*	*Inst*
parallel()	*Inter*	*Inst*
sequential()	*Inter*	*Inst*
skip(final T seed, final UnaryOperator<T> f)	*Inter*	*Inst*
sorted()	*Inter*	*Inst*
sorted(Comparator<? super T> comparator)	*Inter*	*Inst*
unordered()	*Inter*	*Inst*
builder()	*Term*	*Stat*
close()	*Term*	*Inst*
iterator(final T seed, final UnaryOperator<T> f)	*Term*	*Inst*
spliterator()	*Term*	*Inst*
toArray()	*Term*	*Inst*
toArray(IntFunction<A[]> generator)	*Term*	*Inst*

Build operations are the starting point of all streams. Streams can be created out of thin air, via methods such as *generate()*, *of()*, and *iterate()*, or from pre-existing collections such as *stream()* from the *Collection* interface (not shown here). Other pre-existing JDK libraries—including *BufferredReader*, *Files*, *BitSet*, *Pattern*, and *JarFile*, to name a few— also have API methods that generate streams. Streams can also be created from pre-existing streams via *concat()* and can be parallelized very easily with *parallel()* and de-parallelized with *sequential()*. Of course, there are caveats and we'll discuss them later.

Here's a simple, albeit useless, stream:

```
// Create a stream of integers 1, 2, and 3
Stream.of(1, 2, 3);
```

In this example, three integers are being streamed, one at a time, but they fall off the proverbial conveyor belt because there are no other operations processing them. Streams become truly useful when operations are chained together. They have been designed in a style known as *fluent interface*. In Java streams, they are called *pipelines*. The key to pipelining is that methods must always return an instance of themselves and, conveniently, all intermediate stream operations do just that. Any number of intermediate operations can be pipelined. A simple example is:

```
// Store the streamed Integers inside an array
Integer[] integers = Stream.of(1, 2, 3).toArray(Integer[]::new);
```

Here, a stream of three integers is created, passed through the stream, then converted into an array of integers.

Most of the build operations create streams that are backed by physical memory storage. These are said to be finite because they are constrained by physical memory space. But streams can also be created from infinite sources such as *iterate()* and *generate()*. These are said to be infinite streams because elements are generated on the fly. Consider this example:

```
// An infinite stream
Stream.iterate(1, i -> ++i);
```

The *iterate* operation requires a starting point, known as the seed, followed by a function (specifically a *UnaryOperator*) to generate the next element. In this example, the function increments the integer *i*. A sneaky bug arises if we attempt to use a post-increment (*i++*) operator instead of a pre-increment (*--i*) one. Remember that there is no state in the lambda. Once the lambda has incremented *i*, the value is returned to the streams and the integer is destroyed. Thus, a post-increment will not do us any good because it will always return 1.

Iterate operations are the functional programming equivalent of for/while-loops. As such, an exit condition must be provided or the stream will not function properly. An exit condition can be specified by a terminal operation from another family of operations.

Build operations also provide on/off ramps between streams and collections. In this example, we create a stream of integers and store them in an array:

```
// Stream to arrays
Integer[] integers = Stream.of(1, 2, 3).toArray(Integer[]::new);
```

This allows us to leave the world of streams.

Builder operations take this one step further by allowing back-and-forth transitioning. In this next example, we add 100 integers to a stream *builder* object using an imperatively-styled for-loop. Then, we convert back to a stream via the *build()* operation:

```
// Build phase
Stream.Builder<Integer> builder = Stream.builder();
for (int index = 0; index < 100; ++index) {
    builder.add(index);
}

// Build complete
builder.build(); // No more elements can be added at this point
builder.add(101); // Will throw an IllegalStateException
```

The stream *builder* operates like a state machine. First it goes through the build phase, in which elements can be added, and completes with the *build()* method, which turns the builder into a stream. No more elements can be added via *add()* at that point.

We can achieve similar functionality by creating an *ArrayList* and invoking *stream()*. However, the builder offers slightly better performance because the underlying mechanism is still a stream.

Build operations become useful when combined with the other families of operations that we describe next.

Iterate operations

Abstract   Iterate through a stream

Operations

forEach(Consumer<? super T> action)	*Term*	*Inst*
forEachOrdered(Consumer<? super T> action)	*Term*	*Inst*
forEach(Consumer<? super T> action)	*Term*	*Inst*

Iterate operations are always used to terminate streams. They allow for sequential iteration once the element has passed through the stream. The *forEach()* operation can be used this way:

```
// Generate 3 elements and print them
Stream.of(1, 2, 3).forEach(System.out::println);
```

Each element will pass one at the time and be printed with *println()* before the next one is processed—just like a widget passing on a conveyor belt would. There is never more than one widget on the conveyor belt at any one time.

The *forEachOrdered()* operation guarantees to preserve the order if the underlying stream source preserves order (such as with a List). The operation is only relevant for parallel streams. Conversely, *forEach()* makes no effort to preserve order in parallel execution.

Iterate operations are different than build operations because they only iterate over streams—they do not create them. Iterate operations are also terminal.

Filter operations

Abstract   Filter out elements from the stream

Operations

distinct()	*Inter*	*Inst*
filter(Predicate<? super T> predicate)	*Inter*	*Inst*
limit(long maxSize)	*Inter*	*Inst*

Filter operations are the declarative equivalent of *if* statements. They provide a means to remove an element from the stream if it makes it onto the next operation. These are always intermediate operations.

If you conceptualize a filter as being a data net, then its name is a misnomer. *Filter*'s semantics are *"let these go through"* rather than *"filter these out"*. Let's demonstrate its use:

```
// Keep only even numbers and print them
Stream.of(1, 2, 3, 4, 5).filter(i -> i % 2 == 0).
        forEach(System.out::println);
```

The *filter()* operation requires a *Predicate* function. It will filter out all elements passing through it whose condition returns false. In this case, all odd numbers would be removed.

We can combine multiple operations from the *filter* family:

```
// Keep only even numbers and print them
Stream.iterate(1, i -> ++i).limit(10).filter(i -> i % 2 == 0).
    forEach(System.out::println);
```

Since the *iterate()* operation creates an infinite stream, we can use the *limit()* operation to provide an exit condition. The *limit() operation* acts as a short-circuiting operation. This stream will generate integers 1 to 10 and only let even numbers pass through to the *forEach()* operation.

The *distinct()* operation is useful when we want to ensure that duplicate elements are filtered out. For example:

```
// Only print 1, 2, and 3
Stream.of(1, 2, 3, 2, 1).distinct().forEach(System.out::println);
```

The *distinct()* operation is also a minority in that it must keep state in order to determine whether or not the element is distinct. Most operations are stateless.

Map operations

Abstract   Map one value to another of the same or different kind

Operations

flatMap(Function<? super T, ? extends Stream<? extends R>> mapper)	*Inter*	*Inst*
flatMapToDouble(Function<? super T, ? extends DoubleStream> mapper)	*Inter*	*Inst*
flatMapToInt(Function<? super T, ? extends IntStream> mapper)	*Inter*	*Inst*
flatMapToLong(Function<? super T, ? extends LongStream> mapper)	*Inter*	*Inst*
map(Function<? super T, ? extends R> mapper)	*Inter*	*Inst*
mapToDouble(ToDoubleFunction<? super T> mapper)	*Inter*	*Inst*
mapToInt(ToIntFunction<? super T> mapper)	*Inter*	*Inst*
mapToLong(ToLongFunction<? super T> mapper)	*Inter*	*Inst*

Map operations are the heart of any algorithm where computations are performed. This makes them natural intermediate operations. In addition to the generic *map()* and *flatMap()* operations, there are the primitive specializations *flatMapToDouble()*, *flatMapToInt()*, and *flatMapToLong()* and their counterparts *mapToDouble()*, *mapToInt()*, and *mapToLong()*. The *map()* to *flatMap()* dichotomy is based on how they perform their transformation.

The *map()* variants simply perform a one-to-one transformation; they can transform a value on the stream to a different one of the same or different type. This stream doubles every integer as they are passing by:

```
// Double each element of the stream
// Print 2, 4, 6
Stream.of(1, 2, 3).map(i -> i * 2).forEach(System.out::println);
```

We can just as easily transform integers to strings:

```
// Convert the stream from integers to strings describing their
// parity
// Print: "1: odd",   "2: even", "3: odd"
Stream.of(1, 2, 3).
    map(i -> i % 2 == 0 ? i + ": even" : i + ": odd").
        forEach(System.out::println);
```

The stream started as integers and finished as strings. Streams can transform their underlying type any number of times.

The *flatMap()* series of operations is slightly more complex: they transform on a one-to-many basis. For example, this creates a stream of three integers (3, 2, and 1):

```
// Iterate from the current integer to 1 for each stream element
// Print: 3, 2, 1, 2, 1, 1
Stream.of(3, 2, 1).
    flatMap(i ->
        Stream.iterate(i, j -> --j). //Streams can have inner streams
            limit(i)).
                forEach(System.out::println);
```

Each integer gets mapped into n more integers representing the sequence of integers to zero. Notice that the *flatMap()* operation creates its own inner stream, which then gets merged back onto the main stream. Streams can have inner streams.

As we start to build more complex operation pipelines, we need to remember the lexical scoping rules discussed in chapter 4. The lambda defined in the *flatMap()* operation declares integer *i*, which represents the next element of the stream. Its value is used in the lambda body as a parameter to the *iterate()* operation as well as to the *limit()* operation. The variable *i* can no longer be used in other lambdas defined in the pipeline. It's worth repeating that lambdas do not permit variable shadowing. Remember these rules as you construct more elaborate stream pipelines.

Reduce operations

Abstract   Reduce a stream to a single entity

Operations

allMatch(Predicate<? super T> predicate)	Term	Inst
anyMatch(Predicate<? super T> predicate)	Term	Inst
collect(Collector<? super T, A, R> collector)	Term	Inst
collect(Supplier<R> supplier,		
BiConsumer<R, ? super T> accumulator,		
BiConsumer<R, R> combiner)	Term	Inst
count()	Term	Inst
findAny()	Term	Inst
findFirst()	Term	Inst
max(Comparator<? super T> comparator)	Term	Inst
min(Comparator<? super T> comparator)	Term	Inst
noneMatch(Predicate<? super T> predicate)	Term	Inst
reduce(BinaryOperator<T> accumulator)	Term	Inst
reduce(T identity, BinaryOperator<T> accumulator)	Term	Inst
reduce(U identity, BiFunction<U, ? super T, U> accumulator,		
BinaryOperator<U> combiner)	Term	Inst

Reduce operations in general are known as *folds* in functional programming terminology. The idea is to traverse a sequence of values combining ("folding") each with the already traversed portion, concluding with one value at the end. How you combine each is specified with the behavioral parameter. Reduce operations are always terminal because they aggregate entire streams into a single value or object. Let's start by examining the archetype *reduce()* operation. The simplest example is:

```
// Sum integers 1 through 5. Sum will be 15.
int sum = Stream.of(1, 2, 3, 4, 5).reduce(0, (l, r) -> l + r);
```

The *reduce()* operation expects a starting value as well as a *BinaryOperator* acting as an accumulator function. The variable *l* represents the left while *r* is the right. More specifically, the left is the sum of values cumulated thus far while the right is the next element of the stream. This is known as a *left-folding* operation because the list of numbers is traversed from left to right. Right folding operations don't exist natively in the streams API but can be simulated by reversing the order of the elements from the source. The above example is expressed mathematically thusly:

$$(((((0 + 1) + 2) + 3) + 4) + 5) \qquad \{l = 0; r = 1\}$$

$$((((1 + 2) + 3) + 4) + 5) \qquad \{l = 1; r = 2\}$$

$$(((3 + 3) + 4) + 5) \qquad \{l = 3; r = 3\}$$

$$((6 + 4) + 5) \qquad \{l = 6; r = 4\}$$

$$(10 + 5) \qquad \{l = 10; r = 5\}$$

$$15$$

The above example was rigged to guarantee that *sum* would always have a value because we used a variant of *reduce()* that takes an initial value (in this case, 0). What happens if no values from the stream get passed to the *filter()* operation? *Reduce()* will yield nothing:

```
// Sum only even numbers
int sum = Stream.of(1, 3, 5).
          filter(i -> i % 2 == 0).
            reduce((l, r) -> l + r).
              orElse(0);
```

Here, we use a variant of *reduce()*, which returns an *Optional* object. Since only even numbers are considered, our stream may produce nothing. We adjust to this possibility by adding *orElse()*, thereby guaranteeing that *sum* will have a value. Optionals are intrinsic to functional programming because they internalize the results of computation. We've seen many new methods so far in Java 8 that take away the need to inspect the state of an object before deciding what to do. Optionals serve the same purpose.

Optional

Abstract	Provide contingencies when returning values from methods

Methods[4]

T	get()
boolean	isPresent()
void	ifPresent(Consumer<? super T> consumer)
T	orElse(T other)
T	orElseGet(Supplier<? extends T> other)
T	orElseThrow(Supplier<? extends X> exceptionSupplier) throws X
Optional<U>	map(Function<? super T, ? extends U> mapper)
Optional<U>	flatMap(Function<? super T, Optional<U>> mapper)
Optional<T>	filter(Predicate<? super T> predicate)
Optional<T>	*empty()*
Optional<T>	*of(T value)*
Optional<U>	*ofNullable(T value)*

The *Optional* class allow us to put contingencies in place and react appropriately when streams don't produce anything. We can naively invoke *get()* but will face the consequences of a *NoSuchElementException* unchecked exception if the optional contains nothing. A safer way would be to check for the presence of a value using *isPresent()* or only perform an action if a value is present using the *Consumer* variant. A more functional approach would be to use one of the three *orElse()* variants such as *orElseGet()*, which allows us to construct a value, or *orElseThrow()*, which allows us to throw an exception.

Optional offers a rich API that allows us to perform additional streaming on the result. Here we add the numbers but ensure that the result is positive, otherwise 0 is returned. In this example, *filter()* is invoked on the optional:

```
// Ensure the sum is a positive number or return 0
int sum = Stream.of(-20, 2, 4, 6).
    reduce((l, r) -> l + r).filter(i -> i > 0).orElse(0);
```

---

[4] Static methods shown in italics

You can also perform other stream-like operations using *map()*, *flatMap()*, and *of()*. We end this digression of optionals by suggesting, as usual, that you consult the appendix for the complete *Optional* API.

More reduction

Reduce operations can also be used to find things in streams. In that sense, they reduce entire streams to one value. For example:

```
// isPlaceFound will be true
List<String> places =
    Arrays.asList("Villeray", "Plateau", "Rosemont", "Mile-End");
boolean isPlaceFound = places.stream().anyMatch("Rosemont"::equals);
```

The *anyMatch()* operation short-circuits as soon as it finds one condition matching the predicate function. We can also use the more restrictive *allMatch()*, whose condition is to match all.

Closely related are *findFirst()* and *findAny()*. These rely on the existence of a stream value to short-circuit the stream as soon as the first value makes it to that operation. The subtle difference between the two is that *findAny()* is free to return any matching element without regarding encounter order whereas *findFirst()* must respect the order of the stream. We can rewrite the previous example using *findFirst()* instead of *anyMatch()*:

```
// isFound will be true
boolean isFound =

places.stream().filter("Rosemont"::equals).findFirst().isPresent();
```

Mutable reduction

Streams offer multiple ways to perform reduction. This is because reduction is fundamental to algorithms and one size does not fit all. To illustrate the point, let's start with an example that traverses a map containing a population's neighborhoods and their respective population sizes. It streams the map contents, filtering all neighborhoods with population sizes greater than 110K residents:

```
Map<String, Integer> population = new HashMap<>();
population.put("Villeray", 145000);
population.put("Plateau", 100390);
population.put("Rosemont", 134038);
population.put("Mile-End", 31910);

// densesPlaces will be "RosemontVilleray"
String densePlaces =
    population.keySet().stream().
        filter(s -> population.getOrDefault(s, 0) > 110000).
            reduce("", String::concat);
```

The behavioral parameter in the *reduce()* operation receives strings that have passed through the previous *filter()* operation. It returns a concatenated string back to the stream. The stream, in turn, will pass back the structure upon its next element. The problem with this type of reduction is that it does not scale well because it has an expensive accumulator function (e.g., *String::concat*). Its performance would be characterized by the formula $O(n^2)$, where n is the number of characters in the string[5]. In other words, more long strings mean more processing time. Fortunately, there is an alternative for streams with expensive accumulation functions: mutable reduction.

Collect() operations embody the mutable reduction concept. They change the responsibilities of the stream and the behavioral parameter. The stream lets the *collect()* operation's behavioral parameter store each element into a container. The term mutable reduction originates from the fact that containers are mutated as elements are added to it.

Collect() operations work with *suppliers*, *accumulators*, and *combiners*. Suppliers create the containers, accumulators populate the containers, and combiners are only used in parallel execution and ignored by the stream in this example. (We'll cover parallel streams in chapter 8). Let's show an algorithm using a *collect()* operation:

---

[5] This formula is described in big O notation; a mathematical way to express how algorithms behave with ever-increasing data sets. An algorithm with an $O(n^2)$ characteristic scales poorly because as n increases, its processing time grows by a factor of n^2.

```
Map<String, Integer> population = new HashMap<>();
population.put("Villeray", 145000);
population.put("Plateau", 100390);
population.put("Rosemont", 134038);
population.put("Mile-End", 31910);

// densePlaces will contain: "Rosemont", "Villeray"
List<String> densePlaces =
  population.keySet().stream().
    filter(s -> population.getOrDefault(s, 0) >= 110000).
      collect
      (ArrayList::new,                      // Supplier
            ArrayList<String>::add,         // Accumulator
            ArrayList<String>::addAll);     // Combiner

// Some versions of the Java compiler require accumulator to be
// casted
//     collect
//     (ArrayList::new,
//      (BiConsumer<ArrayList<String>, String>)
//       ArrayList<String>::add,
//       ArrayList<String>::addAll);
```

When the first stream element traverses the *collection()* operation, the supplier creates a new *ArrayList*. The element is then added to the accumulator via the *add()*. At the end of the stream's execution, the *ArrayList* is returned, containing all neighborhoods that have passed through the *filter()* operation's predicate.

Collectors can work with any type as long as the supplier creates the object used by the accumulator. As well, the accumulator must be parameterized to match the supplier's and stream's type. Collectors can scale better because they allow more flexibility in how accumulation is done.

There's also a *collect()* variant that works with the *Collector* interface. It allows customized collection implementation to be supplied for advance collecting algorithms. Alternatively, you can use the *Collectors* class to abstract some of these details.

There's a lot more to reduction, including parallelization and re-ordering of elements, that would merit its own chapter or book. We'll limit our discussion and revisit some considerations to make with regards to parallelization in chapter 7.

Peek operations

Abstract   Inject orthogonal, non-interfering behavior into the stream

Operations

peek(Consumer<? super T> action)   *Inter*   *Inst*

The *peek()* operation is useful for injecting orthogonal behavior into the stream. This means any behavior that does not serve nor affect the stream flow. A typical use case is to show stream data for debugging purposes. This can be very useful when constructing long, complex streams. It can show the data as it flows in-between operations:

```
// Inspect the stream values before and after filter
Stream.iterate(1, i -> ++i).
   limit(10).
      peek(i -> { System.out.println("Before filter: " + i); }).
         filter(i -> i % 2 == 0).
            peek(i -> { System.out.println("After filter: " + i);}).
               forEach(System.out::println);
```

Peek operations are mostly harmless because they have no influence on the stream. The *Consumer()* function has no return method and therefore does not affect the flow. However, due to Java's pass-by-reference semantics of objects, it can certainly mutate data as it passes along, just like any other operation. This brings us to the next point of well-behaved streams.

Well-behaved streams

Streams crystalize everything we've discussed so far about functional programming. Java remains flexible in its adherence to functional principles, but with streams you disobey the principles at your own peril. Let's first consider benign cases of badly behaved streams.

Streams must be coherent. That is, they need a build operation, followed by zero or more intermediate ones and capped with a final terminal operation. Incoherent streams, or those that do not follow the prescribed pattern, are useless at best but can have harmful outcomes at worst. Take this example of an incoherent stream:

```
// Incoherent but harmless stream
Stream.of(1, 2, 3, 4, 5).peek(System.out::println);
```

Here, the stream is capped with the intermediate operation *peek()*. Since the stream does not contain a terminal operation, it short-circuits and never performs the peek operation. We need a terminal operation such as this:

```
// findFirst makes this stream coherent
Stream.of(1, 2, 3, 4, 5).peek(System.out::println).findFirst();
```

This example highlights an important property of streams: they can be lazy or eager. Specifically, intermediate operations are lazy while most terminal ones are eager. Every time an intermediate operation is pipelined, it creates a new stream whose data only gets pulled by the next terminal operation. This is why it is characterized as lazy. So pipelining adjacent intermediate operations does nothing without a final terminal operation.

The previous incoherent stream was an example of a finite stream, but streams can also be infinite. In such cases, a terminal operation is also needed to provide an exit. Consider one without such an operation:

```
// Incoherent and harmful stream
Stream.generate(() -> 1).allMatch(i -> i == 1);
```

Here, the generate operation creates an endless supply of integers with a value of one and is pipelined with *allMatch()*, which must inspect the entire infinite set of integers to complete. Needless to say, this stream will execute forever. We need a simple limit operation to make it coherent:

```
// No longer harmful and coherent
Stream.generate(() -> 1).limit(100).allMatch(i -> i == 1);
```

Now, the stream will spew out 100 integers with the value 1.

Non-interference of streams

A well-behaved stream is also one where the stream source is not modified. If the stream originates from a collection, no operation should update it. In fact, most of the time, we're only interested in the elements—not the collection itself. The following is an example of interference:

```
// Never interfere with stream sources like this:
List<String> words =
    new ArrayList<>(
        Arrays.asList("This", "sentence", "contains", "five",
                        "words"));

words.stream().
    forEach(s -> { if (s.equals("five")) words.add("thousand"); });
```

Lambdas supplied to operations should also not have side effects and should be stateless. A lambda whose function has side effects and/or is stateful interferes with the stream's ability to parallelize processing because the elements go through the operation with non-deterministic behavior. The above example is also guilty of having a stateful operation (*words* is a list with state) and has side effects (invoking it can modify its contents and leave *words* in a different state upon the next invocation). Additionally, *ArrayList* is not thread-safe and would require lock management (via *Collections.synchronizedList*). This could also interfere with the efficiency of stream parallelization. Ultimately, not following these guidelines leads to incorrect processing or runtime exceptions. Worse still is that it results in code that is anti-functional in its approach and undermines the whole point of streams.

Streams do maintain state but this is transient state that only exists for the duration of the stream's execution. We've seen examples with *reduction()* operations that maintain state given back to their lambdas. However, there is no usable residual state once the execution terminates. As well, some operations allow stream data to be added or replaced. The reality is that the stream is actually producing new values rather than mutating existing ones. Streams are in tune with functional programming philosophies.

Specialized streams

So far, we've demonstrated by examples using integers as the parameterized type of the stream. In reality, it would have been more convenient to use the specialized stream types to handle integers, longs, or doubles. Each has their own stream type, which are *IntStream*, *LongStream*, and *DoubleStream* respectively. We've seen this pattern in the functional interfaces before with specialized *IntFunction*, *IntConsumer*, *IntPredicate*, and *IntSupplier* as specialized counterparts to *Function*, *Consumer*, *Predicate*, and *Supplier*.

For example, given these two code snippets:

```
// Using the all-purpose Stream to count to 10
Stream.iterate(1, i -> ++i).limit(10).count();

// Using the specialized IntStream to count to 10
IntStream.range(1, 10).count();
```

The *range()* method is preferable because it is more concise and specialized to handle integers. Specialized streams also have their own specialized optional types in *OptionalInt*, *OptionalLong*, and *OptionalDouble*. These are better equipped to handle their respective primitive types because they almost eliminate the need for parameterized types. If nothing else, specialized streams are easier to use because parameterized types sometimes make it impossible for the compiler to infer the type. To overcome this difficulty, casts are sometimes necessary and this makes the code more verbose and harder to read. The specialized *IntStream* gives us the same functionality more concisely.

Additionally, specialized streams offer additional methods. Refactoring a previous example:

```
// Using the all-purpose Stream to sum
int sum = Stream.of(1, 2, 3, 4, 5).reduce(0, (l, r) -> l + r);

// Using the specialized IntStream to sum
IntStream.range(1, 5).sum();
```

The *IntStream* also gives us a class to perform basic statistical analysis. In the next example, we use *IntSummaryStatistics* to compile and print statistics about student test scores:

```java
public static void printTestStats(int[] classOneScores,
                                  int[] classTwoScores) {
    // Convert the arrays into streams to compile statistics
    IntSummaryStatistics classOneStats =
        IntStream.of(classOneScores).summaryStatistics();
    IntSummaryStatistics classTwoStats =
        IntStream.of(classTwoScores).summaryStatistics();


    System.out.println(classOneStats.getMax() + ", " +
                        classOneStats.getMin() + ", " +
                        classOneStats.getAverage() + ", " +
                        classOneStats.getCount());

    System.out.println(classTwoStats.getMax() + ", " +
                        classTwoStats.getMin() + ", " +
                        classTwoStats.getAverage() + ", " +
                        classTwoStats.getCount());

    // Now combine the two
    IntSummaryStatistics combinedStats = new IntSummaryStatistics();
    combinedStats.combine(classOneStats);
    combinedStats.combine(classTwoStats);

    System.out.println(combinedStats.getMax() + ", " +
                        combinedStats.getMin() + ", " +
                        combinedStats.getAverage() + ", " +
                        combinedStats.getCount());
}
```

What's interesting about this class is that we can easily combine the statistics of the two sets of student scores to get aggregated statistics. This is done with the *combine()* method.

Under the hood, *IntSummaryStatistics* is merely a class that extends *IntConsumer*. The stream operation *summaryStatistics()* is a *collect()* operation that creates a new instance of *IntSummaryStatistics* and uses *accept()* as the accumulating function. Thus, *IntSummaryStatistics* is a *consumer* that observes stream elements as they pass through and computes stream statistics. For additional information on the APIs of *IntStream*, *IntSummaryStatistics*, and all variants, consult the appendix.

Wrap up

This completes our high-level overview of streams. We continue with a practical exploration in the next chapter.

Key points

- Streams are the realization of functional programming in Java.

- Streams are a form of declarative-style programming where the focus is on the *what* to do rather than the *how* to do it.

- Streams can be conceptualized as conveyor belts on an assembly line. Workers are operations that perform specific tasks. Widgets are the data passing on the conveyor belt being handled by the workers.

- Streams have operations with pre-defined behavior and are customized via behavioral parameters. These can be expressed through lambdas or method references.

- Stream operations can be grouped into six families: *build*, *filter*, *map*, *reduce*, *iterate*, and *peek*.

- Entire algorithms can be expressed with one or more streams.

- Streams must be coherent and well-behaved.

- Behavioral parameters should be stateless and not interfere with the stream source.

- Streams can also be specialized by primitive type—including integers, longs, and doubles—and offer specialized operations.

Chapter 7: Using Streams

The examples shown in chapter 6 have been short snippets directing the focus on the operations themselves. But streams are powerful enough to encapsulate entire algorithms. They can replace just about any for/while-loop in which data is traversed, sieved, searched, transformed, or condensed. It takes a little practice for the imperative programmer to think in terms of streams rather than for-loops. In this chapter, we'll go through a few examples to demonstrate the thinking process.

Using streams to find prime numbers

In this first example, we'll revisit an algorithm we created in an earlier chapter. We'll write a method that determines whether or not a number is prime. The first example will use an imperative style of programming. We'll then rewrite the algorithm using a declarative form with streams.

The imperative version might look like this:

```java
private static boolean isPrimeImperative(int n) {
    // Treat n == 1 or n == 2 as special cases.
    // Otherwise, assign null to isPrime as a not yet known state
    Boolean isPrime = n <= 1 ? Boolean.FALSE : n == 2
                                  ? Boolean.TRUE : null;

    int limit = (int) Math.sqrt(n);
    for (int i = 2; isPrime == null && i <= limit; ++i) {
        isPrime = n % i == 0 ? Boolean.FALSE : null;
    }

    return isPrime != Boolean.FALSE;
}
```

The first statement treats 1 and 2 as special cases. We hard-code the logic to determine their primeness. Central to this method is the for-loop ensuring that none of the integers divide evenly. This is a prime candidate for streaming. We need to iterate from 2 to the square root of *n*. Also, we need to stop iterating as soon as we encounter a number that divides evenly. That tells us definitely that the number is not prime. We can use an *IntStream* as a for-loop replacement.

Rethinking the above code functionally using streams, we get this:

```java
private static boolean isPrimeStream(int n) {
    // Treat n == 1 or 2 as special cases.
    // Otherwise, assign null to isPrime as a not yet known state
    Boolean isPrime = n <= 1 ? Boolean.FALSE : n == 2 ? Boolean.TRUE
                    : null;

    return isPrime != null ? isPrime :
            IntStream.rangeClosed(2, (int) Math.sqrt(n)).
                noneMatch(i -> n % i == 0);
}
```

We use the *rangeClosed()* operation to create the stream of integers. This operation will iterate from 2 to the rounded down square root of *n* inclusively. We also use the *noneMatch()* reduce operation to ensure that no element streamed divides evenly by a number other than itself.

Now that we have the static method *isPrimeStream()* to find prime numbers, we can easily find the first 100 prime numbers:

```java
// Find the first 100 prime numbers
IntStream.rangeInclusive(1, 100).
    filter(PrimeFinder::isPrimeStream).forEach(System.out::println);
```

We simply iterate over the first 100 numbers and filter out the prime numbers. At the end, we're left with only prime numbers and those are printed.

We can make two observations from this exercise. The first is that imperative code isn't always obvious. We have to follow along the steps to grasp the essence of the code. Declarative-style programming, on the other hand, conveys meaning explicitly. The *rangeInclusive()* operation, in this example, tells us that the stream will produce values from 1 to 100. No need to check for-loop conditions. Likewise, the *filter()* acts as an *if* statement that decides whether or not the next stream element is allowed to continue. Declarative programming puts labels on things and standardizes algorithms. This helps code maintainability.

Second, although not readily apparent in the above example, we can write much more concise code with streams than with loops. While it takes some practice to think in terms of streams, we can write pretty much any algorithm more concisely with streams—just as long as we think in functional terms. Let's gain more practice with streams with a more complex example.

Using streams to find perfect numbers

In number theory, perfect numbers are those whose sum of divisors is equal to the number itself. For example, the number six is a perfect number because:

Divisors of 6 (excluding self): 3, 2, 1

Sum of divisors: 3 + 2 + 1 = 6

By the same token, 8 is **not** a perfect number because:

Divisors of 8 (excluding self): 4, 2, 1

Sum of divisors: 4 + 2 + 1 = 7 (not 8!)

At this time of writing, there are 48 perfect numbers known to mankind. The first four are 6, 28, 496, and 8128; they were discovered thousands of years ago by ancient Greeks mathematicians. Thanks to ever more powerful computers and better software, new perfect numbers are discovered all the time. For example, the most recently discovered perfect number was found in 2013 and was so large that it contained more than 34 million digits!

Let's see how an imperatively-styled perfect number finder would look like:

```java
private static boolean isPerfectImperative(long n) {
    long sum = 0;
    for (long i = 1; i <= n / 2; i++) { // rangeClosed() operation
        if (n % i == 0) {                // filter() operation
            sum += i;                    // reduce() operation
        }
    }

    return sum == n;
}
```

To port this imperative algorithm to a stream-based one, we need to convert each construct into their stream equivalent. The for-loop is a stream operation that creates a stream and iterates over the values with bounds. The *if* statement is a *filter()* operation that only lets certain numbers through for processing. The processing in question is the running sum of the long *i*. The filter's condition is a test for even divisibility. The sum operation is just a reduction in which a bunch of longs iterated over are reduced to one thing—a running sum.

Here's the same code using streams:

```
private static boolean isPerfectStream(long n) {
    return LongStream.rangeClosed(1, n / 2).
        filter(i -> n % i == 0).
            reduce(0, (l, r) -> l + r) == n && n > 0;
}
```

Just as with our prime number finder, our perfect number finder is very concise because we are describing what we want instead of programming how we want it. The for-loop has been replaced with the *rangeClosed()* operation. Here, we simply describe that we want to iterate from 1 to half of n inclusively[6]. The *if* statement has been replaced with a *filter()* operation that only lets evenly divisible numbers through. Then, we sum all evenly divisible numbers with the *reduce()* operation. As we've seen earlier, this operation maintains a running tab represented by the l parameter. Every *long* that satisfies the *filter()* condition will be represented by the r parameter and consequently summed. The result will be remembered by the *reduce()* operation and passed back upon the next cycle via *i*. If no longs satisfy the *filter()* condition, then 0 will be returned as specified by the first parameter of the *reduce()* operation. Finally, if the sum of all evenly divisible numbers is equal to n, and n is greater than 0, *true* is returned. Remember that the *rangeClosed()* and *filter()* operations are intermediate operations. This means that nothing happens until a terminal operation, in this case *reduce()*, pulls the values out of the stream. This underscores the lazy nature streams.

We can now build upon this by checking for the existence of perfect numbers across all longs. Of course, we'd be limited to Java's long type, whose maximum value is 9,223,372,036,854,775,807 and only 19 digits long. Undiscovered perfect numbers are north of 34 million digits long so this algorithm is useful for academic purposes only:

---

[6] It is impossible to find an evenly divisible number that is > n / 2.

```
private static List<Long> findPerfectNumbers(long maxLong,
                                             LongPredicate condition) {
    return LongStream.rangeClosed(1, maxLong).
        filter(condition).
            collect(ArrayList<Long>::new, ArrayList<Long>::add,
                    ArrayList<Long>::addAll);
}
```

Here, we iterate from 1 to *maxLong*—the parameter specified. We also have the condition that is specified by the caller. This is simply *isPerfect* from the previous example. If a number is deemed to be perfect, it is reduced (via the *collect()* operation) and the results are placed in an *ArrayList*. Once *maxLong* is reached, the list of perfect numbers is returned. We can use this method thusly:

```
// Prints 6, 28, 496, 8128
findPerfectNumbers(8128, PerfectNumberFinder::isPerfectStream).
    forEach(System.out::println);
```

Notice that we use the *isPerfect()* method reference as the condition. This will print the first four known perfect numbers, namely 6, 28, 496, and 8128.

Parallel perfect number streaming

Aside from communicating intent more clearly and concisely than the imperatively-styled loops, streams' major selling point is the ease with which they can be parallelized. Here too, developers need not code the *how* to parallelize but the *what* to parallelize. In the simplest cases, one can convert a serial algorithm into a parallel one by simply invoking the *parallel()* operation on streams.

We can continue with the previous *isPerfectStream*() example to show just how easily you can parallelize workflows. It is best to think of the stream parallelization as cloned streams executing side-by-side. As depicted in Figure 10, the *parallel()* operation automatically creates multiple stream pipelines. Each is a cloned pipeline having the operations *filter()* and *reduce()*. There are as many streams created as there are cores on the host's CPU represented by *n* on the diagram.

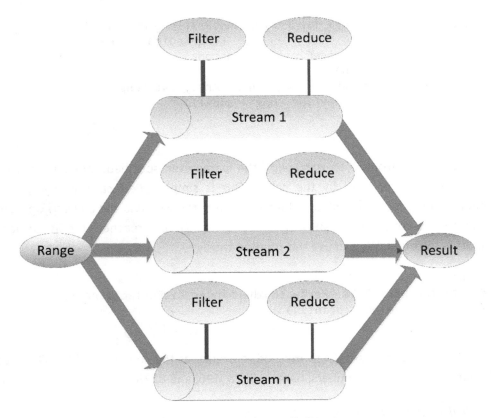

Figure 10: Stream parallelization

Under the hood, streams use the fork-join framework to implement parallelization. Introduced in Java 7, this framework brings core awareness to the JVM by aiming to distribute work evenly amongst all cores available on the host's CPUs. The idea behind the framework is to partition the work to be done, distribute the portions to the available cores, then wait for the result. Streams abstract all of these details but are still bound to the inner workings of the framework.

When the stream in *findPerfectNumbers()* is parallelized, a range of elements is produced and distributed amongst the different pipelines. Each stream pulls the elements through its pipelined operations using a shared thread pool of the fork-join framework.

We can parallelize *isPerfectStream()* like this:

```
private static boolean isPerfectParallel(long n) {
   return
      LongStream.rangeClosed(1, n / 2).
         parallel().
            filter(i -> n % i == 0).
               reduce(0, (l, r) -> l + r) == n && n > 0;
}
```

Streams automatically manage internal state synchronization when parallelized. In this example, the *reduce()* operation maintains a separate sum, which is then aggregated at the end using the same *reduce()* operation. The only change was the addition of the *parallel()* operation after the *rangeClosed()* operation. In reality, it makes no difference where the *parallel()* operation is; once it is added to the pipeline, the entire pipeline is parallelized. The *parallel()* operation merely marks the pipeline as parallel. With this simple addition, numbers can be determined to be perfect in parallel.

We can just as easily parallelize the *findPerfectNumbers()* method:

```
private static List<Long>
   findPerfectNumbers(long maxN, LongPredicate perfectPredicate) {
   return
      LongStream.rangeClosed(1, maxN).
         parallel().
            filter(perfectPredicate).
               collect(ArrayList<Long>::new, ArrayList<Long>::add,
                     ArrayList<Long>::addAll);
}
```

We now invoke *isPerfectParallel()* instead of *isPerfect()*:

```
findPerfectNumbers(8128, PerfectNumberFinder::isPerfectParallel).
   forEach(System.out::println);
```

Notice that we're using the *collect()* operation in *findPerfectNumbers()* to store all longs that have been deemed perfect numbers. Since the stream is parallelized, the third behavioral parameter—the combiner—is used by the stream to combine the lists constructed in parallel. In particular, the *addAll()* method is used as a combiner.

Stream parallelization is a powerful tool but it must be used judiciously. It does not always improve execution. We take a look at this next.

Imperative vs. serial & parallel streaming

Now that we have a serial and a parallel version, we can compare their execution speeds. We can also compare with the original imperative version with which we started.

Number to test	isPerfectImperative	isPerfectStream	isPerfectParallelized
8,128	0	1	0
33,550,336	190	229	66
8,589,869,056	48648	59646	13383
137,438,691,328	778853	998776	203651

Table 2: Execution time in MS (lower is better) [7]

Although unscientific, this table unearths curious facts about streams and how best to use them. Each method was invoked to determine whether or not numbers 8,128, 33,550,336, 8,589,869,056, and 137,438,691,328 are perfect. These are, in fact, all perfect numbers chosen to ensure the algorithm executes fully without short-circuiting. With small numbers like 8,128, the execution delay is below one millisecond so implementations are interchangeable. However, there are significant differences as numbers become bigger. As one would expect, the serialized stream version does not scale well for huge work sets. The parallelized version, making efficient use of multi-core technology, utilizes all cores and performs much faster. For 12-digit numbers, it executes in one fifth of the time compared to the serialized version. But perhaps more interesting is the fact that the imperative version, not using streams, is faster than the serialized one. So when should we use imperatively-styled loops, serialized streams, or parallelized streams? We can better answer this question if we break it down into two questions: imperatively-styled loops vs. functional streams and serial vs. parallel streams.

Imperative loops vs. functional streams

By now you have seen that you can convert just about any loop into one or more stream pipelines. But does that mean that you should make wholesale use of streams in your

---

[7] Executed on an Intel i7 920, 2 quad-core CPUs, 2.67Ghz, 64-bit, 9GB RAM, Win 7.

code base? In Java, we live in a legacy world where streams did not exist from the outset. This means that as Java developers, we will be maintaining code written with for/while-loops. Introducing streams in a legacy application will require some planning. Will every member of the team understand this new paradigm? Will every member be comfortable using streams? Should the code remain consistent and stream-free until best practices are brought forth? Is it better to introduce streams gently in a brand new code base? From this pragmatic perspective, you may choose to avoid streams. You can decide for yourself by considering these pros and cons.

Streams pros are:

- **They are declarative constructs:** With streams, you code the *what* and not the *how* of looping constructs. This is the Ikea approach to programming where constructs, like Ikea furniture, come pre-fabricated and customization comes from how they are combined with others.
- **Communication of intent:** Streams communicate behavior intent effectively. This is superior to custom imperatively-styled loops where intent can be obfuscated by a developer's limited skill level, peculiar habits, or error. Once you master streams, you will know which stream operation to use and communicate your intent succinctly to other developers.
- **Conciseness:** Since the actual looping code is not coded, you are removing the plumbing code. Streams yield less code.
- **Easier to test**: Since streams yield less code, code written with streams is easier to test and the plumbing itself does not need to be tested. As well, streams are functional constructs and functional programming in general is better able to be proved correct because of its emphasis on immutability and functional purity.
- **On-demand parallel streaming**: Streams allow you to switch to parallel execution with one operation. You simply cannot get this with imperative loops.

Streams cons are:

- **Density**: The dark side of conciseness is code density. As code becomes more powerful it becomes more dense and more difficult to parse. Streams do tend to be more dense than imperative for-loops and require a trained eye to parse.
- **Loss of flexibility**: Declarative constructs by their very nature require you to give up control. In this sense, you will not be able to control flow exactly as you have been accustomed. For example, you cannot mutate local variables of the

method enclosing the stream. With regular loops, local variables are in the same lexical scope and can therefore be mutated. Functional programming and streams impose their own way of doing things and this will result in a loss of flexibility until this paradigm is well understood.

- **Loss of efficiency**: Closely related to the previous point is the fact that sometimes, when you yield control to a framework or library that generalizes behavior, you may lose efficiency. We saw this in our perfect number finder where the imperative version executed faster than the serial counterpart. Over time, frameworks can get smarter about processing and pass on the gains to its users. Garbage collection is one such example where there was an initial loss of efficiency when compared to manual memory management, followed by subsequent gains as garbage collectors became smarter.

If Java generics introduced in Java 5 can serve as a precursor, this author's bet is that we will live in a heterogeneous world for a very long time. Streams will become mainstream in Java programming but many developers will remain untrained and avoid them altogether.

Serial vs. parallel streams

This is a much more interesting question. We have purposefully ignored the potential pitfalls of parallel streams until now. Like any infomercial, anytime something seems too good to be true, it usually is. After all, if concurrent programming were so easy, our industry wouldn't assign the development of concurrent code to the most capable hands. The reality is that streams and functional programming do offer a better mousetrap for concurrency but you have to play by the rules. Not all problems fit neatly with these rules and so not all problems can be solved with parallel streams.

In our discussion of well-behaved streams, we listed the rules for stream parallelization. To recapitulate, streams must have operations that are stateless and have no side effects. In addition, parallel streams work best when your code abides by these rules:

- **Must fit the associativity property:** Since execution order cannot be guaranteed in parallel streams, we must ensure that the associativity property is respected. This is expressed mathematically as:
  - $((a + b) + c) = (a + (b + c))$

For example, when we used reduce operations in our perfect number finders, the sum function was associative in that order did not matter. But had the algorithm required subtraction instead of addition, we could not have used parallel streams because subtraction is not associative.

- **ROI on parallelization overhead**: The laws of concurrency apply just like in the real world. It is very easy to activate parallelization with streams but enough code must run in parallel to justify the overhead. Otherwise, there will be no return on investment and parallel execution will actually be slower.
- **Processing is CPU-bound:** Adding to the previous point, stream parallelization works best on CPU-bound processing, that is, processing that is CPU-intensive and requires no I/O. Ideally, parallel streams are used after lists have been constructed from external sources (e.g., database queries, user input, network calls, etc.) and ready to be processed.
- **Thread saturation:** Since streams use the fork-join framework, having multiple levels of streams, such as a parent stream calling a child stream, will work off of the same thread pool. So care must be given to not over-parallelize stream processing.

The examples in this chapter were well-behaved and their performance improved when we introduced stream parallelization. There was no stream source interference, no stateful operations, and no side effects. With the associative reduction operation using summation, there was sufficient processing to warrant the overhead of the fork-join framework. In fact, the very nature of finding perfect numbers is a classic example of a CPU-bound algorithm. While real-life examples will tend to be more complex and nuanced, the perfect number finder is the mold to follow in designing a well-behaved stream.

Stream parallelization has the potential to make developers mindless in their use of parallelization. Armed with this powerful new toy, developers can try to micro-optimize every line of code by introducing parallelization. Fortunately, the price to pay to switch from serial to parallel is nominal. But if your problem does not play nice with these rules, there is no shame in using serial streams.

Wrap up

This completes our overview of streams. There is much more we could discuss. An entire book can be dedicated exclusively to streams. In this respect, we have barely scratched the surface. Still, you now have a good understanding of what is possible with streams and should start using them in the real world. Streams require a little practice because they demand a new way of looking at algorithms. There are also some more caveats and we'll look at these in chapter 8.

Key points

- Streams can replace almost any for/while-loop provided we think in functional terms.

- Streams should not necessarily be used as a wholesale replacement for all looping constructs. There are pros and cons for their use.

- Stream usage pros are that they are declarative, yield concise code, communicate intent clearly, and offer an easy path to parallelization.

- Stream usage cons are that they can create dense code, remove flexibility, and be less efficient.

- Streams can be parallelized but only work when algorithms fit the associativity property. Processing can be made more efficient if there is enough code to parallelize and the nature of the algorithm is CPU bound.

- Streams parallelization should not be abused because performance can be degraded.

Part IV
Finale

Chapter 8: Thinking functionally

We've now covered all the new key features related to functional programming in Java 8. If you're a Java developer, learning functional programming in Java will feel like learning to drive a car with manual transmission when your only experience is with an automatic one. At first, your previous experience with driving will hurt as much as help because you will have to re-learn all the basics: how to accelerate, how to pass at high speeds, and how to stay idle. You'll also need to think about new things: how to brake using engine compression, how to park on an incline, and how to avoid crashing into the car behind you when starting on an incline.

The objective of this book is to guide the transition of the imperative, object- oriented Java developer to the new functional world. It would feel incomplete without a final chapter expanding upon the topics covered in previous chapters. I want to tie loose ends, raise new questions, and let you come to your own conclusions as you explore Java 8 and functional programming further. Some topics are complex enough to warrant their own book while some just need a paragraph, such as logging.

Logging

We start with an easy topic. Introducing functional programming as a brand new tool in Java 8 will spark major changes in the Java world. After all, lambdas facilitate the whole *behavior-as-data* pattern. Although anonymous functions offer the same feature, their clumsiness takes the fun out of it. In the end, we are not drawn to think in those terms and our classes are designed differently. But what if it is now much easier to pass behavior around? One such plebeian example is the way logging would be redesigned if behavior could be easily passed to methods. In a world without lambdas, we do this:

```
logger.fine("My debug log: " + myObject.getState());
```

If, however, executing *getState()* and concatenating with *"my debug log"* is expensive, we use this idiom, also known as a log guard, to maximize efficiency:

```
if (logger.isLoggable(Level.FINE)) {
    logger.fine("My debug log: " + myObject.getState());
}
```

Now, we only get the state and concatenate if we know for sure it will be logged. The problem is that this idiom is just lipstick on a pig. We have to litter our codebase with countless *if* statements. What we really have is an abstraction leak because the caller shouldn't even be concerned with such things.

We can redesign this API much better with Java's standard functional interfaces. Using a *Supplier* functional interface, we can log this way:

```
logger.fine(() -> "My debug log: " + myObject.getState());
```

With this, the string is only assembled if the log level corresponds to fine. It is concise and efficient and puts the responsibility back where it belongs: in the Logger.

Lambdas allow us to take a lazy approach to code execution. We don't have to eagerly assemble the log line until we know for sure that the string concatenation will actually be used. So obvious is this design that it should come as no surprise that Java's logger API has been enriched exactly this way. Expect all 3rd-party logging frameworks to offer something identical.

Design Patterns

The previous is one small example of how API designs change when behavior-as-data comes to the forefront. When you think about it, many of the Design Patterns from the Gang of Four are about standardizing, communicating, and facilitating behavior-as-data. In fact, all of the creation patterns (Abstract Factory, Builder, Factory Method, Prototype, and Singleton) are nothing more than constructs that return behavior. Isn't that what lambdas are all about?

Design Patterns helped the industry's adoption of Java and object-oriented programming. Java did not have an easy mechanism allowing for code to define code (behavior-as-data). Likewise, objected-oriented programming didn't formalize these concepts. Design Patterns stepped in to bridge the gap. With lambdas in Java, all bets are off with respect to the importance and stature of the classic Design Patterns.

This is a complex topic that merits its own book and you can expect many future debates about the need for Design Patterns in the new functional Java world. At this juncture, know that any pattern whose sole purpose is to determine behavior is at risk of becoming outdated and irrelevant. Most of the creational patterns, by their very nature of being in the behavior-as-data business, are in this at-risk group. The Design Patterns book also defines structural patterns (Adapter, Bridge, Composite, Decorator, Façade, Flyweight, and Proxy) and behavioral patterns (Chain of Responsibility, Command, Interpreter, Iterator, Mediator, Memento, Observer, State, Strategy, Template Method, and Visitor) and these may also be at risk. In the very least, they can be simplified to the point where they are one-liners masquerading as complex feats of software engineering.

To illustrate the point, let's start with the Factory Method creational pattern:

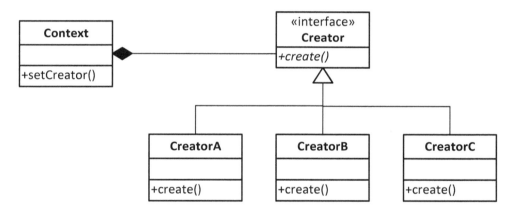

Figure 11: Factory Method Design Pattern

The pattern requires a *creator* interface to define the *create* method, allowing subclasses to implement concrete methods. If we're using some kind of dependency injection framework, we wire one of the concrete *Creator* implementations to our *Context* object. At some point, it will invoke the *create()* method on the injected instance. In code, this could look like this:

```
interface Creator {
    public Object create();
}
```

```
public class CreatorA implements Creator {
    @Override
    public Object create() {
        // Simplified logic
        return new MyObject();
    }
}
```

If we need to wire the classes manually, we can do this:

```
// Set the creator to A
context.setCreator(new CreatorA());
```

With Java 8, we can use the standard *Supplier* functional interfaces to achieve the same.

Figure 12: Supplier functional interface

And manually wire thusly:

```
context.setSupplier(() -> new MyObject());
```

Where has all the glue code gone? Can we even call this a design pattern anymore? By using standard functional interfaces and a lambda in Java 8, we have eliminated most of the code and have communicated intent succinctly.

A similar fate awaits some behavioral patterns. Think of the strategy pattern whose sole purpose is to pass behavior around. Its design is as such:

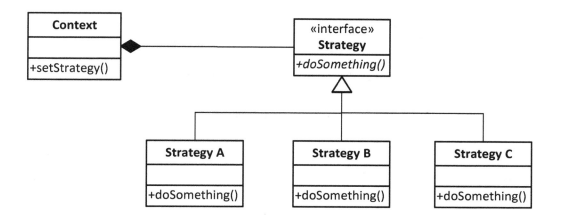

Figure 13: Strategy Design Pattern

The patterns compel the class designer to create an interface, in this case *Strategy*, along with a method that triggers an action, in this case, *doSomething()*. After, any new code variations require the sub-classing of *Strategy* and a concrete definition of code in *doSomething()*:

```
interface Strategy {
    public void doSomething(Object context);
}


public class StrategyA implements Strategy {
    @Override
    public void doSomething(Object context) {
        // Do something
    }
}
```

We manually wire the classes together like this:

```
// Set the strategy to A
context.setStrategy(new StrategyA());
```

With Java 8, we can use the standard *Consumer* interfaces to achieve the same.

Figure 14: A functional Strategy Design Pattern

Code wise, we just have:

```
context.setConsumer<Object> consumer  = o -> { /* Do something*/ };
```

Can we call this one-liner a design pattern anymore? Both Factory Method and Strategy patterns have been drastically reduced in size.

The popular Decorator pattern is another casualty of functional programming. This pattern enables behavior to be dynamically assembled at runtime—something that cannot be done by sub-classing.

Conceptually, the decorator pattern looks like this:

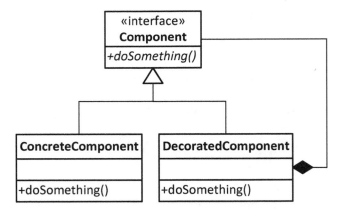

Figure 15: The Decorator Design Pattern

Omitting the verbose code needed to implement this pattern, we skip right to the Java 8 version using functional composition to achieve the same thing:

```
Function<Object, String> decoratedFunction =
        s -> s + ", then do this first";
Function<Object, String> function =
        s -> s + ", then do this after";

System.out.println(function.compose(decoratedFunction)
                .apply("Start"));

// Output:
// Start, then do this first, then do this after
```

And we can re-assemble the function to reverse the order:

```
System.out.println(function.andThen(decoratedFunction)
                    .apply("Start"));

// Output:
// Start, then do this after, then do this first
```

Or, we can keep the same output as the first example by reversing the order of invocation of *decoratedFunction* and *function* and using *andThen()*. This is because given any *Function* instance *x* and *y*, *x.compose(y)* is equal to *y.andThen(x)*.

```
// Equal to function.compose(decoratedFunction).apply("Start")
System.out.println(decoratedFunction.andThen(function)
                                .apply("Start"));

// Output:
// Start, then do this first, then do this after
```

In brief, we see a diminished importance of Design Patterns in Java 8; there is simply no need for an over-engineered pattern when the same idea can be expressed with a one-line lambda. However, Design Patterns whose focus is on state management rather than pure behavior remain useful. Examples of these are the Command, Memento, and Observer patterns. Of course, if you're adhering to functional design principles, you're avoiding, minimizing, and confining state and so will rely on these less often. Java has become a hybrid of objected-oriented programming and functional programming so classic Design Patterns still have their place—but only for code that is designed in an objected-oriented way.

The idea of formalizing common constructs is still useful in functional programming but it needs to start at a higher level of abstraction to be useful—just like functional programming itself. While there are patterns being created for functional programming, there is still no definitive authority. Let's hope a definitive book, such as the Gang of Four's book, emerges for functional programming. For now, let's discuss one commonly used construct in functional programming to give you a taste of how they might differ for the classic Design Patterns.

Currying

The functional world already has its own ways of doing things. Whenever we visit new worlds, the proper first step is to learn how the practitioners do things. One example that figures prominently is the concept of *currying*. Named after the renowned mathematician Haskell Curry, whose name was also lent to the Haskell functional programming language, currying is the concept of transforming a function that takes multiple arguments in such a fashion that it can be called multiple times each with single-argument invocations. It has its roots in mathematics and was partly developed by Haskell Curry himself. It's a fundamental technique used in purely functional languages whose functions, like lambda calculus, are limited to being single-argument functions. This technique allows functions that require multiple arguments to be invoked as a series of single-argument functions. The Java language does not have this limitation because it is not an abstraction of lambda calculus. It therefore derives no benefit from currying used that way. However, it is useful in the context of a functional design pattern.

Currying is best explained with concrete code:

```
// Subtraction using currying
IntFunction<IntFunction<Integer>> subtraction = x -> y -> x - y;
System.out.println(subtraction.apply(5).apply(4));

// Prints 1
```

In this simple example, we use currying to subtract 4 from 5. Currying works in tandem with the concept of higher-order functions. Higher-order functions are simply functions that return other functions. In the Java world, this could mean that a method returns one of the standard functional interfaces such as *Function* or any variant in the *Function* family. In the above example, *subtraction* is defined as a lambda that returns a lambda (or an *IntFunction* that returns an *IntFunction*) and is an illustration of a higher-order function. The invocations of *apply()* are said to be *curried* because the result of the *apply(5)* is curried to invoke *apply(4)*. You can do this repeatedly as long as the function invoked returns a function.

There is something quite surprising going on if we look closely. With the invocation of *subtraction.apply(5),* the lambda returned is:

```
y -> 5 - y;
```

The number 5 is embedded within the lambda. The variable x has now become the value 5. When the *apply(4)* is invoked, the *y* variable is replaced with 4, yielding 5 − 4. Currying allows lambdas to be parameterized.

There is little use for this type of currying in Java; this is a convoluted way of subtracting two numbers. But currying does have its place when used to parameterize behavior at multiple levels. Suppose that we wanted to build a function to translate a number into its string representation. Suppose further that we wanted to add a second level of varying behavior: the strategy used to translate would differ by language. So given a language and numbers zero to nine, the function would return a string representing numbers in that language. Let's see how this would look in code:

```
Function<String, Function<Integer, String>>
    checker = language -> numberedWord -> {
      switch (language) {
        case "English" : {
          return Arrays.asList("Zero", "One", "Two", "Three",
                "Four", "Five", "Six", "Seven", "Eight", "Nine")
                .get(numberedWord % 10);
        }

        case "French" : {
          return Arrays.asList("Zéro", "Un", "Deux", "Trois",
                "Quatre", "Cinq", "Six", "Sept", "Huit", "Neuf")
                .get(numberedWord % 10);
        }

        case "Italian" : {
          return Arrays.asList("Zero", "Uno", "Due", "Tre",
                "Quatro", "Cinque", "Sei", "Sette", "Otto",
                "Nove").get(numberedWord % 10);
        }

        default: {
          return "???";
        }
      }
    }
};
```

Once defined, we invoke *checker* like this:

```
// Currying in Java
System.out.println(checker.apply("English").apply(2));
System.out.println(checker.apply("French").apply(8));
System.out.println(checker.apply("Italian").apply(7));
System.out.println(checker.apply("Klingon").apply(9));

// Prints "Two", "Huit", "Sette", "???"
```

Let's look at this code through a microscope. We start by the declaration of *checker*:

```
Function<String, Function<Integer, String>>
    checker = language -> numberedWord -> {…}
```

The variable *checker* is a *Function* that returns another *Function* (a higher-order function). The first step is:

```
checker.apply("English")
```

This step sets the language variable value to "English" in lambda. This is used in the *switch* statement. We then curry the result with:

```
checker.apply("English").apply(1);
```

With the *language* variable set to "English", the switch statement will now choose the "English" case and invoke the *get* in that list of words. We can change the translation behavior per language.

In general terms, currying is useful when not all parameters are known at once. For example, we can wire the language at start-up time and apply the number to translate later in the program. In a way, this is a functionalized version of the Factory Method and Strategy patterns we saw earlier.

Natively functional languages can more naturally express curried algorithms as they are embedded into the syntax. In some languages, it is also a matter of necessity. Java, on the other hand, expresses currying through a functional design pattern approach. Through it, functional thinking can be manifested and can bring forth all the benefits of functional programming. We'll see more currying in the next example.

Stretching Java to its functional limits

So now that Java has been functionalized, can it be said to be on a level playing field with newer languages built functionally from the ground up? As previously mentioned, Java is a hybrid mix of imperative programming and objected-oriented programming with functional flavorings. It can be used functionally but due to its legacy, it cannot do everything that a strongly functional language can do. This is neither good nor bad. We use different tools for different things and we don't define functional programming to be good and everything else to be bad. But let's say we are strong proponents of functional programming and wanted to go all in. Would Java support or limit us? Would it break under stress? Let's explore with an example.

We will take the quick sort algorithm and re-implement it in a functional way using Java 8 tools. The textbook quick sort is a good example of imperative thinking and shows us the bumps we'll hit when trying to go functional. As you do this exercise, you will face two kinds of challenges:

- Rewiring your imperative brain to a functional one
- Getting around some of the Java limitations

Let's see what these are. As you'll recall from your college days, the quick sort algorithm works this way:

1. Find the midpoint of a given array, which we'll call the pivot.
2. Determine all values that are less than the pivot on the left side and all those greater on the right side and swap the lower with the higher until the comparison reaches the pivot.
3. Split the array at the pivot and repeat the process recursively for both halves.
4. Repeat the entire process until each sub-array can no longer be split.

Here's the quick sort algorithm written in an imperative style:

```java
public static ArrayList<Integer>
    imperativeQuickSort(ArrayList<Integer> array, int low, int n) {
    int lo = low;
    int hi = n;

    if (lo >= n) {
        return array;
    }

    // Step 1: find pivot point
    int mid = array.get((lo + hi) / 2);

    // Step 2: find & swap values less & greater than pivot
    while (lo < hi) {
        while (lo < hi && array.get(lo) < mid) {
            lo++;
        }
        while (lo < hi && array.get(hi) > mid) {
            hi--;
        }
        if (lo < hi) {
            // Swap values
            int temp = array.get(lo);
            array.set(lo, array.get(hi));
            array.set(hi, temp);
            lo++;
            hi--;
        }
    }

    if (hi < lo) {
        lo = hi;
    }

    // Steps 3 & 4: split the array and repeat recursively
    imperativeQuickSort(array, low, lo);
    imperativeQuickSort(array, lo == low ? lo + 1 : lo, n);

    return array;
}
```

Looking at this code, we notice three hallmarks of imperative programming:

- The externalization of loops (e.g., while-loop)

- The manipulation of state (e.g., lo++, hi--)
- Verbosity

The *while* is an externalized loop and uses *lo* and *hi* state changes to control the flow. Both of these are incompatible with functional programming and will have to be re-thought. As well, imperative programming is usually more verbose than its functional counterpart. We don't want to change for the sake of being functional but rather to reap the benefits of functional programming, namely:

- **Internalize loops with streams:** Streams communicate intent more clearly and succinctly. They also enable easy parallelization.
- **Avoid state mutation:** It is easier to reason with immutable code.
- **Minimize code:** Having less code performing the same functionality reduces probability of error and makes it easier to understand and maintain.

Let's address all three points. Here's our first attempt at converting this quick sort algorithm into a functional style:

```
public static List<Integer> functionalSort(List<Integer> array) {
    List<Integer> returnArray = array;

    if (array.size() > 1) {
        // Step 1
        int mid = array.get(array.size() / 2);

        // Step 2
        Map<Integer, List<Integer>> map = array.stream().
            collect(Collectors.groupingBy(
                    i -> i < mid ? 0 : i == mid ? 1 : 2));

        // Steps 3 & 4
        List<Integer> left =
            functionalSort(
                    map.getOrDefault(0, new ArrayList<>()));
        List<Integer> middle = map.getOrDefault(1,
                    new ArrayList<>());
        List<Integer> right =
            functionalSort(map.getOrDefault(2, new ArrayList<>()));

        left.addAll(middle);
        left.addAll(right);

        returnArray = left;
    }

    return returnArray;
}
```

The while-loops in step 2 have been replaced by a single stream statement. This brevity is a typical outcome of converting external loops into internal ones. However, a consequence is that we lose fine-grained control of what is done inside the loop. In particular, notice that we can't manipulate the *lo* and *hi* states like we did in the imperative version. We can try to contort the stream into manipulating state but the outcome will be ugly and go against the grain of functional thinking. A better solution is to re-think step 2 functionally.

Viewed holistically, step 2 iterates over the entire sub-array it has been given and ensures that all values on the left are smaller than the pivot and that all those on the right are greater. For that, we can use a reduction stream operation and organize the sub-array into buckets. They will contain:

- **Bucket 0:** numbers less than the pivot
- **Bucket 1:** numbers equal to the pivot
- **Bucket 2:** numbers greater than the pivot

We do this with the *collect()* operation. We use the *groupingBy()* method from the *Collectors* utility class as a shorthand. It converts the stream integer element into both an index for a map and the map itself. Once the entire sub-array has been streamed, we have a map with one to three buckets, each containing the list of integers that are less than, equal to, and greater than the pivot, respectively.

The next step is to recursively sort each of the buckets until they can no longer be split. As the stack unwinds for each sub-array, *left*, *middle*, and *right* are merged together. The end result is that the entire method is sorted with no state mutation other than the merging of lists. We have achieved the first two objectives: internalize loops and avoid state mutation. The third objective has only been partly achieved: the process of merging is still a little verbose.

If we look at the cause, verbosity stems from the fact that each bucket's sub-array is stored inside a list. Then, that list is merged with the other two buckets. It takes a total of six lines of code to implement step 3. Part of the problem is due to Java's object-oriented DNA. Lists are meant to be created and interacted with as a series of calls within a conversation. This is a hallmark of object-oriented programming. Using the fluent interface style, as adopted by streams, leads to code that is more concise and more aligned to functional programming. Here, however, the two styles are at odds. The *addAll()* statement prevents us from chaining multiple statements as a pipeline because it does not return the merged list itself but rather a *Boolean* to indicate the results of the merge. This was a deliberate design choice of Java's syntax and we often see this in the standard libraries. The end result is that the fluent interface style is inhibited.

Ideally, our code would look like this:

```
// Steps 3 & 4 using a fluent interface style
// Does not compile
return functionalSort(map.getOrDefault(0, new ArrayList<>())).
    addAll(map.getOrDefault(1, new ArrayList<>())).
        addAll(functionalSort(map.getOrDefault(2,
            new ArrayList<>()))));
```

Of course, this is not possible. However, we can simulate a fluent interface style with currying. Here's how:

```
private static final
    Function<List<Integer>,
                Function<List<Integer>,
                Function<List<Integer>, List<Integer>>>> merge =
                    left -> middle -> right -> {
                        left.addAll(middle);
                        left.addAll(right);
                        return left;
                    };

public static List<Integer> curriedSort(List<Integer> array) {
    if (array.size() > 1) {
        int mid = array.get(array.size() / 2);

        Map<Integer, List<Integer>> map = array.stream().
            collect(Collectors.groupingBy(
                    i -> i < mid ? 0 : i == mid ? 1 : 2));

        // Use currying to merge the 3 buckets together
        Return merge.apply(
                curriedSort(map.getOrDefault(0, new ArrayList<>())))
                .apply(map.getOrDefault(1, new ArrayList<>()))
                .apply(curriedSort(map.getOrDefault(2,
                        new ArrayList<>())));
    }
    else {
        return array;
    }
}
```

The entire quick sort algorithm has been re-written and shown in the *curriedSort()* method. First, we define a higher-order function named *merge()*. It has three levels of lambdas. Since we don't know what the *left*, *middle*, and *right* lists will be at the outset, we use currying to replace each parameter as it becomes known. Once they are all known, the final merged list is returned. In this example, currying fulfills two important roles:

- It bridges the object-oriented *addAll()* with the functional sort
- It simulates the fluent interface style

Now, step 3 can be expressed in one line.

Let's review the outcome of this refactoring exercise. We have achieved the first two objectives of internalizing loops and minimizing state mutation. However, the third objective of reducing verbosity was a partial success. When compared to functional languages with native support, Java code is still more verbose. For example, this code could have been written more concisely in Scala. Why does Java code end up being more verbose? Let's look at the reasons:

- **Lambdas are backed by functional interfaces:** The compiler needs to see the functional interface defined in order to understand what type of lambda it is and what can be done with it. Witness the verbose *merge()* type definition.
- **Functional interfaces are often generic:** This yields code that is much more verbose.
- **Lack of fluent interface style support in Java syntax and libraries:** This requires that we adopt a more object-oriented style or use techniques like currying to simulate it.
- **Non-native support for functional programming:** Lambdas are the only native functional constructs in Java 8. Every other functional construct is achieved through libraries or functional Design Patterns. The lack of native support results in more verbose code as seen in the quick sort example.

Another important point is how well intent is communicated. The curried sort resulted in code that was much more dense than its imperative version and this is a typical result. Code density is a double-edged sword: it can reduce footprint but can also be harder to understand. In the case of step 2, streams communicated intent more clearly than several while-loops could. Once we understand what the *collect()* operation does, we know we are streaming values into buckets. This is reusable knowledge that transcends the quick sort algorithm. While-loops, on the other hand, are always custom and intent needs to be understood every time. In the case of step 3, the call is harder to make. Java's limitations necessitated a more complex approach. A case can be made for favoring either *functionalSort()* or *curriedSort()*. However, compared to *imperativeQuickSort()*, both functional versions resulted in more elegant and concise code that communicated intent more clearly than their imperative counterpart.

Incidentally, the imperative quick sort performed better than either of the functional versions. These findings are consistent with those discussed in chapter 7 when comparing the perfect number finder written in an imperative style vs. two stream-based versions. The trade-offs discussed in that chapter are relevant to the quick sort comparisons as well.

This exercise also demonstrates the full functional thinking buy-in required to get that quality code. Next, we look at how Java fairs in recursively expressed algorithms.

Recursion

Recursion is an important tool in strongly functional languages because it models lambda calculus and other mathematical constructs. Proper support is expected; the language should allow any algorithm to be expressed recursively. In fact, functional purists will only recognize a language to be functional based on how well it supports recursion. Of course, full support is difficult for any programming language because of physical limitations; every recursive iteration consumes memory in the form of stack frames. Stack frames are records that store incoming parameters, local method variables, and return addresses needed once the method has completed. Functional languages, designed for heavy use of recursion, can be optimized. Tail-call optimization is one such example that allows memory used for local variables to be released if the last operation is a recursive call (or even a call to another method). This makes sense because if it can be proven by the compiler or runtime that the local variable is no longer needed, it can be released prematurely and safely. Furthermore, the return address can be removed because it is no longer needed when the stack unwinds. It can be replaced by a goto-like instruction that returns control to the address where recursion started. With no more local variables and return addresses, even the stack itself can be bypassed. Essentially, you get all the elegance of a recursive algorithm without the stack footprint.

Consider this method that recursively computes *n* factorial. It is a prime candidate for tail-call optimization:

```java
private static long classicFactorial(long n, long accumulate) {
    return n == 1 ? accumulate :
                    classicFactorial(n - 1, n * accumulate);
}
```

In a tail-call optimized language, this method should work for very large numbers. In Java byte code, the last operation is the recursive invocation to itself. Unfortunately, the

Java Virtual Machine does not support tail-call optimization. Running the above code will exhaust the stack some time after 10000 recursions (depending on your JVM configuration). The Java Virtual Machine is a host to functional languages such as Scala, Groovy, and Clojure and this limitation affects these languages as well. Requests have been made to support this optimization. However, they have gone unanswered because there is a good deal of complexity involved and it is not important enough for Java's agenda.

Fortunately, if you really need industrial-grade recursion, there are software workarounds. One such technique is *trampolining*. Trampolining simulates recursion but takes away the consumption of the stack. It preserves all the elegance of recursion without the costs and limitations.

Here's the factorial example using trampolining:

```java
// Factorial using trampolining
public class TrampoliningInJava {
    private static Supplier<?> factorial(BigInteger n,
            BigIntegerWrapper sum) {
        sum.holder = sum.holder.multiply(n);
        return n.intValue() > 1 ?
            () -> factorial(n.subtract(BigInteger.ONE), sum) : null;
    }

    private static class BigIntegerWrapper {
        BigInteger holder = BigInteger.valueOf(1);
    }

    public static void main(String[] args) {
        // Define the trampoline consumer function
        Consumer<Supplier<?>> trampoline = supplier -> {
            while (supplier != null) {
                supplier = (Supplier) supplier.get();
            }
        };

        // Works with very large numbers
        BigIntegerWrapper wrapper = new BigIntegerWrapper();
        trampoline.accept(
                factorial(BigInteger.valueOf(15000), wrapper));
        System.out.println(wrapper.holder);
    }
}
```

TrampoliningInJava allows the recursive design to remain intact. We define the *factorial* method as a recursive algorithm but instead of letting *factorial* make the recursive call itself, it returns a *supplier* function that makes a call to itself when invoked. It lets the *trampoline Consumer* function act as a middle man triggering the invocation. This is key to avoid using the stack. Notice as well that *trampoline* is method signature agnostic; *factorial* can have any number or type of parameters as long as it returns a *supplier*. Since we lose the opportunity to return the running product of the *factorial*, we use a *BigIntegerWrapper* to pass along that product and mutate it along the way. We've also changed the parameter type to a *BigInteger* to calculate astronomical factorials.

The method now works for very large numbers because it uses simulated recursion. You can define the *trampoline Consumer* function once in your project and put it in a shared interface or class.

Having said all that, if you don't like the extra code, you can always avoid recursive implementations altogether. You can use a stream pipeline to get the job done:

```java
// Factorial using streams
private static BigInteger streamFactorial(long n) {
    return Stream.
        iterate(BigInteger.valueOf(n), next ->
                next.subtract(BigInteger.ONE))
                .limit(n).reduce(BigInteger::multiply).get();
}
```

Deciding which option is best is an exercise left to the reader.

Key points

- Thinking functionally requires you to re-learn the basics.

- Logging is a prime example of how functional thinking can improve an API.

- Design Patterns can be eliminated or modernized with functional programming.

- Functional programming requires Design Patterns to operate at a higher level of abstraction.

- Currying works with higher-order functions and partial application. It allows functions to be invoked one parameter at a time as they become known.

- Currying can be used to implement functional Design Patterns.

- Imperative algorithms must be rethought to fit the functional model.

- Java supports functional thinking but its lambda form can make it more verbose than other functional languages.

- Java is not a tail-call optimized language but trampolining can be used to support industrial-grade recursion.

Chapter 9: Conclusion

This completes my analysis of functional programing in Java 8. Writing this book has been my journey as much as yours and we now see code in a whole new way. I hope you feel compelled to go out and use Java 8. As with any new tool, you will need to judge for yourself how to best leverage it and decide which applications could benefit and which will not. As you gain a deeper understanding of functional programming, you might be tempted to use it as a magic bullet. Should you now eschew object-oriented principles in favor of functional programming? Will your workplace even adopt Java 8 and will you get buy-in from all stakeholders? And what about the eight million other Java developers worldwide? Will they embrace or shun the changes? Finally, what's in store for Java 9 and beyond? Will Java become even more functional or will this experiment fail and push Java to the margins? Here are my thoughts.

The functional programming panacea

Just because functional programing tools exist doesn't mean we need to use them all the time. Throughout this book, I have tried to abstain from promoting the use of functional programming for its own sake. Use should be based on its own merit. But this is easier said than done. Our industry is just as fad-oriented as the fashion industry.

I remember back in the early days of Java the introduction of Enterprise Java Beans (EJBs). In the late 1990s, Java was the cool new kid on the block and the addition of EJBs as part of the Enterprise Edition made everyone in the Java community a little crazy. If your application did not use EJBs, there was something wrong with you. Being a contrarian meant you were being left out of the party. It took a few years for best practices to emerge and what followed was a violent anti-EJB backlash from which EJBs never recovered. Entity beans in particular, a subset of EJBs that focused on persistence, were obliterated from the enterprise. What lessons did that teach us?

- The wisdom of the crowd is not always filled with wisdom
- Fads come and go
- Being a contrarian is no fun

You can expect functional programming to become even more popular with the release of Java 8. There are now better ways to do things in Java. But Java remains a hybrid of different programming models. Use the right tools for the job. Resist the movement of the masses!

Workplace adoption

Your workplace might be slow to upgrade to Java 8. After all, it is an upgrade like no other. It must be introduced with care. I remember my own experience of introducing Java 5 to a former workplace. There was some resistance to Java 5 because developers had to be familiarized with the use of auto boxing, new for-loops, var args, static imports, and generics, the most complex new feature. Yet, these additions are now dwarfed by those of Java 8. If this experience is to serve as a model, developers will need to be trained to effectively use functional programming. Generics remain poorly understood and under-utilized many years later.

The stakes are much higher for Java 8 but at least it brings much more to the table. Generics, possibly the most important change of previous releases, offer much less to overall code quality than does Java 8's functional programming. Generics are about type safety and a harder sell to management because the improvements in code are rather subtle. Java 8's selling points are much more tangible, namely: declarative programming, emphasis on immutability, conciseness, and a better way to parallelize processing. This translates into efficient use of CPU power and noticeable improvements on overall code quality, all contributing to the bottom line. This should motivate workplace adoption.

Another force will be the embracing of functional APIs by 3rd party libraries. Expect many Java libraries to be functionalized. This will motivate organizations to upgrade to access the new and revamped libraries. This will also expose Java developers to functional ideas. A basic understanding of the lambda syntax and concepts will be required to use these APIs. Some developers will progress and become more proficient and start functionalizing their own internal APIs when it makes sense. A subset of that group will become fully-functional human beings as they adopt advanced functional concepts. If generics are to serve as a model, educating the masses will take many years.

If you want to introduce Java 8 in your workplace but face resistance, let the need to access 3rd-party library updates be the driving force. Libraries using Java 8 constructs and provided as a jar cannot run on a Java 7 (or previous) runtime. Unlike generics, previous versions of Java are not forward-compatible with lambda-related byte code.

You can, however, upgrade to a Java 8 runtime and run pre-Java 8 code without modification. Let this little fact do the heavy lifting for you. Once Java 8 has entered your workplace, you will be able to use lambdas and the new standard libraries.

Community acceptance

The software industry is becoming increasingly fragmented with organizations adopting more diverse technologies and heterogeneous programming environments. Some organizations have already moved onto new languages to get their functional fix because Java did not support functional programming. Will Java 8 bring them back? Only time will tell but here are some thoughts. Java remains a top-tier language consistently ranking as one of the most popular programming languages in world. Its installed base alone can dictate where things will go. I remain skeptical that features added to Java 8 will satisfy functional purist programming with more functional languages. In that way, Java will not make great advances in capturing that mindshare. However, in terms of offering the huge user base better tools, I think Java 8 has succeeded. That will guarantee that Java remains relevant for a long time to come. I do think that the Java community will adopt the functional principles but it will take years.

Java 9 and beyond

Java 8 is just the first step in a series of planned releases. The language architects have promised that Java will be even more functional with future releases. If Java 8 is to serve as a model, I think we're going to exciting new places. The future is bright for Java!

Appendix

The standard functional interfaces

Consumer			
Synopsis	**Consume & discard**		
Functional interface	**Type[8]**	**Return**	**Method**
Consumer<T>	Abs	void	accept(T t);
	Def	Consumer<T>	andThen(Consumer<? super T> after);
BiConsumer<T, U>	Abs	void	accept(T t, U u);
	Def	BiConsumer<T, U>	andThen(BiConsumer<? super T, ? super U> after);
DoubleConsumer	Abs	void	accept(double value);
	Def	DoubleConsumer	andThen(DoubleConsumer after);
IntConsumer	Abs	void	accept(T t);
	Def	IntConsumer	andThen(IntConsumer after);
LongConsumer	Abs	void	accept(long value);
	Def	LongConsumer	andThen(LongConsumer after);
ObjDouble Consumer<T>	Abs	void	accept(T t, double value);
ObjIntConsumer<T>	Abs	void	accept(T t, int value);
ObjLong Consumer<T>	Abs	void	accept(T t, long value);
Function			
Synopsis	**Transform/Compute**		
Functional interface	**Type**	**Return**	**Method**
Function<T, R>	Abs	R	apply(T t);
	Def	Function<V, R>	compose(Function<? super V, ? extends T> before);
	Def	Function<T, V>	andThen(Function<? super R, ? extends V> after);
	Stat	Function<T, T>	identity();
BiFunction<T, U, R>	Abs	R	apply(T t);
	Def	BiFunction<T, U, V>	andThen(Function<? super R, ? extends V> after);
BinaryOperator<T>	Stat	BinaryOperator<T>	minBy(Comparator<? super T> comparator);

---

[8] **Abs**: Abstract method, **Def**: Default method, **Stat**: Static method

	Stat	BinaryOperator<T>	maxBy(Comparator<? super T> comparator);
DoubleFunction<R>	Abs	R	apply(double value);
DoubleToInt Function	Abs	Int	applyAsInt(double value);
DoubleToLong Function	Abs	Long	applyAsLong(double value);
IntFunction<R>	Abs	R	apply(int value);
IntToDouble Function	Abs	Double	applyAsDouble(int value);
IntToLongFunction	Abs	Long	applyAsLong(int value);
LongFunction<R>	Abs	R	apply(long value);
LongToDouble Function	Abs	double	applyAsDouble(long value);
LongToInt Function	Abs	int	applyAsInt(long value);
ToDoubleBi Function<T, U>	Abs	double	applyAsDouble(T t, U u);
ToDouble Function<T>	Abs	double	applyAsDouble(T value);
ToIntBiFunction	Abs	int	applyAsInt(T t, U u);
ToIntFunction	Abs	int	applyAsInt(T value);
ToIntBi Function<T, U>	Abs	long	applyAsLong(T t, U u);
ToLongFunction<T>	Abs	long	applyAsLong(T value);
DoubleBinary Operator	Abs	double	applyAsDouble(double left, double right);
DoubleUnary Operator	Abs	double	applyAsDouble(double operand);
	Def	DoubleUnary Operator	compose(DoubleUnaryOperator before);
	Def	DoubleUnary Operator	andThen(DoubleUnaryOperator after);
	Stat	DoubleUnary Operator	identity();
IntBinaryOperator	Abs	int	applyAsInt(int left, int right);
IntUnaryOperator	Abs	int	applyAsInt(int operand);
	Def	IntUnary Operator	compose(IntUnaryOperator before);
	Def	IntUnary Operator	andThen(IntUnaryOperator after);
	Stat	IntUnary Operator	identity();

LongBinary Operator	Abs	long	applyAsLong(long left, long right);
LongUnaryOperator	Abs	long	applyAsLong(long operand);
	Def	LongUnary Operator	compose(LongUnaryOperator before);
	Def	LongUnary Operator	andThen(LongUnaryOperator after);
	Stat	LongUnary Operator	identity();
UnaryOperator<T>	Stat	Unary Operator<T>	identity();
Predicate			
Synopsis	**Test/Filter**		
Functional interface	**Type**	**Return**	**Method**
Predicate<T>	Abs	boolean	test(T t);
	Def	Predicate<T>	and(Predicate<? super T> other);
	Def	Predicate<T>	negate();
	Def	Predicate<T>	or(Predicate<? super T> other);
	Stat	Predicate<T>	isEqual(Object targetRef);
BiPredicate<T, U>	Abs	boolean	test(T t);
	Def	BiPredicate <T, U>	and(BiPredicate<? super T, ? super U> other);
	Def	BiPredicate <T, U>	negate();
	Def	BiPredicate <T, U>	or(BiPredicate<? super T, ? super U> other);
DoublePredicate	Abs	boolean	test(double value);
	Def	Double Predicate	and(DoublePredicate other);
	Def	Double Predicate	negate();
	Def	Double Predicate	or(DoublePredicate other);
IntPredicate	Abs	boolean	test(int value);
	Def	IntPredicate	and(IntPredicate other);
	Def	IntPredicate	negate();
	Def	IntPredicate	or(IntPredicate other);
LongPredicate	Abs	boolean	test(long value);
	Def	LongPredicate	and(LongPredicate other);
	Def	LongPredicate	negate();
	Def	LongPredicate	or(LongPredicate other);
Supplier			
Synopsis	**Create**		

Functional interface	Type	Return	Method
Supplier	Def	T	get();
BooleanSupplier	Def	boolean	getAsBoolean()
DoubleSupplier	Def	double	getAsDouble();
IntSupplier	Def	int	getAsInt();
LongSupplier	Def	long	getAsLong();
Comparator			
Description	**Test two objects for equivalence**		
Functional interface	**Type**	**Return**	**Method**
Comparator<T>	Abs	int	compare(T o1, T o2);
	Def	Comparator<T>	reversed();
	Def	Comparator<T>	thenComparing(Comparator<? super T> other);
	Def	Comparator<T>	thenComparing (Function<? super T, ? extends U> keyExtractor, Comparator<? super U> keyComparator);
	Def	Comparator<T>	thenComparing(Function<? super T, ? extends U> keyExtractor);
	Def	Comparator<T>	thenComparingInt (ToIntFunction<? super T> keyExtractor);
	Def	Comparator<T>	thenComparingLong (ToLongFunction<? super T> keyExtractor);
	Def	Comparator<T>	thenComparingDouble (ToDoubleFunction<? super T> keyExtractor);
	Stat	Comparator<T>	reverseOrder();
	Stat	Comparator<T>	naturalOrder();
	Stat	Comparator<T>	nullsFirst(Comparator<? super T> comparator;
	Stat	Comparator<T>	nullsLast(Comparator<? super T> comparator);
	Stat	Comparator<T>	comparing(Function<? super T, ? extends U> keyExtractor, Comparator<? super U> keyComparator);
	Stat	Comparator<T>	comparing(Function<? super T, ? extends U> keyExtractor);

	Stat	Comparator<T>	comparingInt(ToIntFunction<? super T> keyExtractor);
	Stat	Comparator<T>	comparingLong(ToLongFunction<? super T> keyExtractor);
	Stat	Comparator<T>	comparingDouble(ToDoubleFunction<? super T> keyExtractor);

The Stream Interface

Build			
Synopsis	**Create a stream**		
Variants	**IntStream, LongStream, DoubleStream**		
Return	**Method**	**Cont/type[9]**	**Synopsis**
Stream<T>	concat(Stream<?extends T> a, Stream<? extends T> b)	Intr/Stat	Concatenates two streams to form a new one.
Stream<T>	empty()	Intr/Stat	Creates an empty stream.
Stream<T>	generate(Supplier<T> s)	Intr/Stat	Creates a stream based on the given *supplier.*
Stream<T>	iterate(final T seed, final UnaryOperator<T> f)	Intr/Stat	Iterate through a stream from a starting point using *f* to generate the next element.
Stream<T>	of(T t)	Intr/Stat	Creates a stream of one element of type *T.*
Stream<T>	of(T... values)	Intr/Stat	Creates a stream of one or more element of type *T.*
S	onClose(Runnable closeHandler)	Intr/Inst	Returns an equivalent stream with an additional *closeHandler.*
S	parallel()	Intr/Inst	Returns a parallel representation of the stream.
S	sequential()	Intr/Inst	Returns a sequential representation of the stream.
Stream<T>	skip(long n)	Intr/Inst	Discard the first *n* elements and returns the remainder of the stream.
Stream<T>	sorted()	Intr/Inst	Sorts the stream based on its natural order.

---

[9] Continuity/Type: Continuity=**Intr**: Intermediate, **Term**: Terminal
Type=**Inst**: Instance, **Stat**: Static

Stream<T>	sorted(Comparator<? super T> comparator)	Intr/Inst	Sorts the stream based on the given comparator.
S	unordered()	Intr/Inst	Returns an unordered stream
Builder<T>	builder()	Term/Stat	Returns a builder allowing the stream to be mutated.
void	close()	Term/Inst	Closes this stream, causing all close handlers for this stream pipeline to be called.
Iterator <T>	iterator()	Term/Inst	Returns an *iterator*.
Spliterator <T>	spliterator()	Term/Inst	Returns a *spliterator*.
Object[]	toArray()	Term/Inst	Converts the stream into an array of *Object* objects.
A[]	toArray(IntFunction<A[]> generator)	Term/Inst	Converts the stream into an array of *A* based on an *IntFunction*.

Iterate			
Synopsis	**Traverse a stream**		
Return	**Method**	**Cont/Type**	**Synopsis**
void	forEach(Consumer<? super T> action)	Term/Inst	Iterates through the stream applying the *Consumer* to each element.
void	forEachOrdered (Consumer<? super T> action)	Term/Inst	Iterates through the stream applying the *Consumer* function to each element and guaranteeing the order of the stream if the stream has one.

Filter			
Synopsis	**Filter stream elements**		
Return	**Method**	**Cont/Type**	**Synopsis**
Stream<T>	distinct()	Intr/Inst	Filters out duplicate elements and creates a new stream.
Stream<T>	filter(Predicate<? super T> predicate)	Intr/Inst	Filters elements of the stream based on the predicate condition.

Map			
Synopsis	**Transform elements of the stream**		
Return	**Method**	**Cont/Type**	**Synopsis**

Stream<R>	flatMap(Function<? super T, ? extends Stream<? extends R>> mapper)	Intr/Inst	Returns a *Stream* consisting of the results of replacing each element of this stream with the contents of the stream produced by applying the provided mapping function to each element.
Double Stream	flatMapToDouble (Function<? super T, ? extends DoubleStream> mapper)	Intr/Inst	Returns a *DoubleStream* consisting of the results of replacing each element of this stream with the contents of the stream produced by applying the provided mapping function to each element.
IntStream	flatMapToInt(Function<? super T, ? extends IntStream> mapper)	Intr/Inst	Returns an *IntStream* consisting of the results of replacing each element of this stream with the contents of the stream produced by applying the provided mapping function to each element.
Long Stream	flatMapToLong (Function<? super T, ? extends LongStream> mapper)	Intr/Inst	Returns a *LongStream* consisting of the results of replacing each element of this stream with the contents of the stream produced by applying the provided mapping function to each element.
Stream<R>	map(Function<? super T, ? extends R> mapper)	Intr/Inst	Returns a *Stream* consisting of the results of applying the given function to the elements of this stream.
Double Stream	mapToDouble(ToDoubleFunction<? super T> mapper)	Intr/Inst	Returns a *DoubleStream* consisting of the results of applying the given function to the elements of this stream.
Int Stream	mapToInt(ToIntFunction<? super T> mapper)	Intr/Inst	Returns an *IntStream* consisting of the results of applying the given function to the elements of this stream.

Long Stream	mapToLong(ToLongFunction<? super T> mapper)	Intr/Inst	Returns a *LongStream* consisting of the results of applying the given function to the elements of this stream.
Reduce			
Synopsis	**Reduce the stream to a value**		
Return	**Method**	**Cont/Type**	**Synopsis**
boolean	allMatch(Predicate<? super T> predicate)	Term/Inst	Returns true if all elements in the stream match the *Predicate* condition.
boolean	anyMatch(Predicate<? super T> predicate)	Term/Inst	Returns true if at least one element in the stream matches the *Predicate* condition.
R	collect(Collector<? super T, A, R> collector)	Term/Inst	Aggregates the stream using the collector providing functions for each step of the collection process.
R	collect(Supplier<R> supplier, BiConsumer<R, ? super T> accumulator, BiConsumer<R, R> combiner)	Term/Inst	Aggregates the stream using a *Supplier, Accumulator,* and *Combiner.*
long	count()	Term/Inst	Counts the elements in the stream.
Optional <T>	findAny()	Term/Inst	Returns any element in the stream as an *Optional*. Does not necessarily return the first element.
Optional <T>	findFirst()	Term/Inst	Returns the first element of the stream as an *Optional*.
Optional <T>	max(Comparator<? super T> comparator)	Term/Inst	Returns the maximum value in the stream as defined by the *Comparator.*
Optional <T>	min(Comparator<? super T> comparator)	Term/Inst	Returns the minimum value in the stream as defined by the *Comparator.*
boolean	noneMatch(Predicate<? super T> predicate)	Term/Inst	Returns true if no element in the stream matches the *Predicate* condition.
Optional <T>	reduce(BinaryOperator<T> accumulator)	Term/Inst	Aggregates the stream as one value.

Return	Method	Cont/Type	Synopsis
T	reduce(T identity, BinaryOperator<T> accumulator)	Term/Inst	Aggregates the stream as one value using *T* as the starting value.
U	reduce (U identity, BiFunction<U, ? super T, U> accumulator, BinaryOperator<U> combiner)	Term/Inst	Aggregates the stream as one value using *T* as the starting value and a combiner operator for parallel operations.
Synopsis	**Inspect the stream elements without disturbing the stream**		
Return	**Method**	**Cont/Type**	**Synopsis**
Stream<T>	peek(Consumer<? super T> action)	Intr/Inst	Performs the action defined in the consumer for each element in the stream without affecting the stream.

The IntStream Interface

Build			
Synopsis	**Create a stream**		
Variants	**Stream, LongStream, DoubleStream**		
Return	**Method**	**Cont/type[10]**	**Synopsis**
IntStream	concat(IntStream a, IntStream b)	Intr/Stat	Concatenates two streams to form a new one.
IntStream	empty()	Intr/Stat	Creates an empty stream.
IntStream	generate(IntSupplier s)	Intr/Stat	Creates a stream based on the given *IntSupplier*.
IntStream	iterate(final int seed, final IntUnaryOperator f)	Intr/Stat	Iterates through a stream from a starting point using *f* to generate the next element.
IntStream	of(int t)	Intr/Stat	Creates a stream of one int of value *t*.
IntStream	of(int... values)	Intr/Stat	Creates a stream of ints represented by *values*.
IntStream	range(int startInclusive, int endExclusive)	Intr/Stat	Creates a stream of ints from *startInclusive* to *endExclusive* exclusively.
IntStream	rangeClosed(int startInclusive, int endInclusive)	Intr/Stat	Creates a stream of ints from *startInclusive* to *endInclusive* inclusively.
Double Stream	asDoubleStream()	Intr/Stat	Converts the stream into a stream of doubles.
Long Stream	asLongStream()	Intr/Stat	Converts the stream into a stream of longs.
Stream \<Integer\>	boxed()	Intr/Stat	Converts the stream into a stream boxed into Integer.
S	onClose(Runnable closeHandler)	Intr/Stat	Returns an equivalent stream with an additional *closeHandler*.
IntStream	parallel()	Intr/Inst	Returns a parallel representation of the stream.
IntStream	sequential()	Intr/Inst	Returns a sequential representation of the stream.
IntStream	skip(long n)	Intr/Inst	Discards the first *n* elements and returns the remainder of the stream.
IntStream	sorted()	Intr/Inst	Sorts the stream based on its natural order.

[10] Continuity/Type: Continuity=**Intr**: Intermediate, **Term**: Terminal
Type=**Inst**: Instance, **Stat**: Static

Builder	builder()	Term/Stat	Returns a builder allowing the stream to be mutated.
void	close()	Term/Inst	Closes this stream, causing all close handlers for this stream pipeline to be called.
Primitive Iterator. OfInt	iterator()	Term/Inst	Returns an *iterator*.
Spliterator .OfInt	spliterator()	Term/Inst	Returns a *spliterator*
int[]	toArray()	Term/Inst	Converts the stream into an array of ints.

	Iterate		
Synopsis	**Traverse a stream**		
Return	**Method**	**Cont/Type**	**Synopsis**
void	forEach(IntConsumer action)	Term/Inst	Iterates through the stream applying the *IntConsumer* to each element.
void	forEachOrdered (IntConsumer action)	Term/Inst	Iterates through the stream applying the *IntConsumer* function to each element and guaranteeing the order of the stream if a stream has one.
Synopsis	**Filter stream elements**		
Return	**Method**		**Synopsis**
IntStream	distinct()	Intr/Inst	Filters out duplicate elements and creates a new stream.
IntStream	filter(Predicate<? super T> predicate)	Intr/Inst	Filters elements of the stream based on the predicate condition.
IntStream	limit(long maxSize)	Intr/Inst	Returns a stream consisting of the elements of this stream, truncated to be no longer that maxSize.

	Map		
Synopsis	**Transform elements of the stream**		
Return	**Method**	**Cont/Type**	**Synopsis**

Return	Method	Cont/Type	Synopsis
IntStream	flatMap(IntFunction<? extends IntStream> mapper)	Intr/Inst	Returns an *IntStream* consisting of the results of replacing each element of this stream with the contents of the stream produced by applying the provided mapping function to each element.
IntStream	map(IntUnaryOperator mapper)	Intr/Inst	Returns an *IntStream* consisting of the results of applying the given function to the elements of this stream.
Double Stream	mapToDouble (IntToDoubleFunction mapper)	Intr/Inst	Returns a *DoubleStream* consisting of the results of applying the given function to the elements of this stream.
Long Stream	mapToLong(ToLongFunction<? super T> mapper)	Intr/Inst	Returns a *LongStream* consisting of the results of applying the given function to the elements of this stream.
Stream <U>	mapToObj(IntFunction<? extends U> mapper)	Intr/Inst	Returns an object-valued Stream consisting of the results of applying the given function to the elements of this stream.
Reduce			
Synopsis	**Reduce the stream to a value**		
Return	**Method**	**Cont/Type**	**Synopsis**
boolean	allMatch(IntPredicate predicate)	Term/Inst	Returns true if all elements in the stream match the *Predicate* condition.
boolean	anyMatch(IntPredicate predicate)	Term/Inst	Returns true if at least one elements in the stream matches the *Predicate* condition.
Optional Double	average()	Term/Inst	Returns the average value of the stream.
R	collect(Supplier<R> supplier, ObjIntConsumer<R> accumulator, BiConsumer<R, R> combiner)	Term/Inst	Aggregates the stream using a *Supplier, Accumulator,* and *Combiner.*
long	count()	Term/Inst	Counts the elements in the stream.

Optiona lInt	findAny()	Term/Inst	Returns any element in the stream as an *Optional*. Does not necessarily return the first element.
Optiona lInt	findFirst()	Term/Inst	Returns the first element of the stream as an *Optional*.
Optional <T>	max()	Term/Inst	Returns the maximum value in the stream.
Optional <T>	min()	Term/Inst	Returns the minimum value in the stream.
boolean	noneMatch (IntPredicate predicate)	Term/Inst	Returns true if no element in the stream matches the *Predicate* condition.
Optional Int	reduce(IntBinaryOperator op)	Term/Inst	Aggregates the stream as one value.
int	reduce(int identity, IntBinaryOperator op)	Term/Inst	Aggregates the stream as one value using identity as the starting value.
int	sum()	Term/Inst	Adds all the elements of the stream.
Int Summary Statistics	summaryStatistics()	Term/Inst	Returns an *IntSummaryStatistics* describing various summary data about the elements of this stream.
Peek			
Synopsis	Inspect the stream elements without disturbing the stream		
Return	Method	Cont/Type	Synopsis
IntStream	peek(IntConsumer action)	Intr/Inst	Performs the action defined in the consumer for each element in the stream without affecting the stream.

The functionalized Collections library

A list of methods added to key interfaces in the Collections library in Java 8.

Collection		
Return	**Method**	**Synopsis**
boolean	removeIf(Predicate<? super E> filter)	Removes the element if the predicate condition is true.
Spliterator <E>	spliterator()	Creates a spliterator from the collection.
Stream<E>	stream()	Creates a stream from the collection.
Stream<E>	parallelStream()	Creates a parallel stream (if possible) from the collection.
List (extends Collection)		
Return	**Method**	**Synopsis**
void	sort(Comparator <? super E> c)	Sorts the list using the comparator.
void	replaceAll(UnaryOperator <E> operator)	Replaces each element of this list with the result of applying the operator to that element.
Spliterator <E>	spliterator()	Creates a spliterator from the list.
Set (extends Collection)		
Return	**Method**	**Synopsis**
Spliterator <E>	spliterator()	Creates a spliterator from the set.
Map		
Return	**Method**	**Synopsis**
void	forEach(BiConsumer<? super K, ? super V> action)	Performs the given action on each entry in this map.
void	replaceAll(BiFunction<? super K, ? super V, ? extends V> function)	Replaces each entry's value with the result of invoking the given function on that entry.
V	getOrDefault (Object key, V defaultValue)	Returns the value to which the specified key is mapped or *defaultValue* if none mapped.
V	putIfAbsent(K key, V value)	Puts the element if absent.
V	computeIfAbsent (K key, Function<? super K, ? extends V>	Puts the value generated by the mapping function if the key is absent.

	mappingFunction)	

V	computeIfPresent
	(K key,
	  BiFunction<? super K,
	    ? super V,
	    ? extends V>
	  remappingFunction)
		If the value for the specified key is present and non-null, attempts to compute a new mapping given the key and its current mapped value.

V	compute
	(K key,
	  BiFunction<? super K,
	    ? super V,
	    ? extends V>
	  remappingFunction)
		Attempts to compute a mapping for the specified key and its current mapped value or null if there is no current mapping.

V	merge
	(K key, V value,
	  BiFunction<? super V,
	    ? super V,
	    ? extends V>
	  remappingFunction)
		If the specified key is not already associated with a value or is associated with null, associates it with the given value.

boolean	remove(Object key, Object value)	Removes the entry for the specified key only if it is currently mapped to the specified value.

boolean	replace(K key,
	    V oldValue,
	    V newValue)
		Replaces the entry for the specified key only if it is currently mapped to the specified value.

V	replace(K key, V value)	Replaces the entry for the specified key only if it is currently mapped to some value.

Iterator		
Return	Method	Synopsis
void	forEachRemaining (Consumer<? super E> action)	Performs the given action for each remaining element in the order in which elements occur when iterating.

Iterable		
Return	Method	Synopsis
void	forEach (Consumer<? super T> action)	Performs the given action on the contents of the Iterable in the order in which elements occur when iterating.
Spliterator<T>	spliterator()	Creates a spliterator from the iterable.

The Optional Interface

Optional		
Synopsis	**Provide contingencies when returning values from methods.**	
Variants	**OptionDouble, OptionalInt, OptionalLong**	
Return	**Method**	**Synopsis**
T	get()	Returns the value contained in the *Optional* if present; otherwise throws a *NoSuchElementException*
void	ifPresent (Consumer<? super T> consumer)	Invokes the *Consumer* if present; otherwise does nothing
boolean	isPresent()	Returns true if a value is present in this *Optional*; otherwise returns false
T	orElse(T other)	Returns the value contained in this *Optional* if present; otherwise returns *other*
T	orElseGet (Supplier<? extends T> other)	Returns the value contained in this *Optional* if present; otherwise invokes other to generate a value
T	orElseThrow (Supplier<? extends X> exceptionSupplier) throws X	Returns the contained value if present; otherwise throws an exception to be created by the provided supplier
Optional <U>	map(Function<? super T, ? extends U> mapper)	Applies the provided *mapper* if a value is present. If the result is non-null, returns an *Optional*; otherwise returns an empty *Optional*.
Optional <U>	flatMap (Function<? super T, Optional<U>> mapper)	Applies the provided *mapper* if a value is present. If the result is non-null, returns an *Optional*; otherwise returns an empty *Optional*.
Optional<T>	filter(predicate<? super T> predicate)	Returns an Optional if a value is present and matches the given *predicate*; otherwise returns an empty *Optional*
Optional<T>	empty()	Returns an empty *Optional* instance
Optional<T>	of(T value)	Returns an *Optional* with the specified present non-null value
Optional <U>	ofNullable(T value)	Returns an *Optional* describing the specified value if non-null; otherwise returns an empty *Optional*

The OptionalInt Interface

OptionalInt		
Synopsis	**Provide contingencies when returning values from methods.**	
Variants	**Optional, OptionalDouble, OptionalLong**	
Return	**Method**	**Synopsis**
int	get()	Returns the value contained in the *OptionalInt* if present; otherwise throws a *NoSuchElementException*.
void	ifPresent(IntConsumer consumer)	Invokes the *IntConsumer* if present; otherwise does nothing.
boolean	isPresent()	Returns true if a value is present in this *OptionalInt*; otherwise returns false.
int	orElse(int other)	Returns the value contained in this *OptionalInt* if present; otherwise returns *other*.
int	orElseGet(IntSupplier other)	Returns the value contained in this *OptionalInt* if present; otherwise invokes other to generate a value.
int	orElseThrow (Supplier<X> exceptionSupplier) throws X	Returns the contained value if present; otherwise throws an exception to be created by the provided supplier.
Optional Int	empty()	Returns an empty *OptionalInt* instance.
Optional Int	of(int value)	Returns an OptionalInt with the specified present non-null value.

Bibliography & References

[Gam95] Gamma Erich, Richard Helm, Ralph Johnson, John Vlissides. Design Patterns: Elements of Object-Oriented Software. Addison-Wesley.

[Tate10] Bruce A. Tate, Seven Languages in Seven Weeks, Pragmatic Bookshelf.

[Hortsmann12] Cay Stat. Horstmann, Scala for the Impatient, Addison-Wesley.

[Hindley06] J. R. Hindley, F. Cardone, History of λ-calculus and Combinatory Logic, Swansea University Mathematics Department Research Report

[Ford11-13] Neal Ford, Functional Thinking, Developer Works,
- Thinking functionally, Part 1, http://www.ibm.com/developerworks/java/library/j-ft1/index.html
- Thinking functionally, Part 2, http://www.ibm.com/developerworks/java/library/j-ft2/index.html
- Thinking functionally, Part 3, http://www.ibm.com/developerworks/java/library/j-ft3/index.html
- Immutability, http://www.ibm.com/developerworks/java/library/j-ft4/index.html
- Coupling and composition, Part 1, http://www.ibm.com/developerworks/java/library/j-ft5/index.html
- Coupling and composition, Part 2, http://www.ibm.com/developerworks/java/library/j-ft6/index.html
- Functional features in Groovy, Part 1, http://www.ibm.com/developerworks/java/library/j-ft7/index.html
- Functional features in Groovy, Part 2, http://www.ibm.com/developerworks/java/library/j-ft8/index.html
- Functional features in Groovy, Part 3, http://www.ibm.com/developerworks/java/library/j-ft9/index.html
- Functional design patterns, Part 1, http://www.ibm.com/developerworks/java/library/j-ft10/index.html
- Functional design patterns, Part 2, http://www.ibm.com/developerworks/java/library/j-ft11/index.html
- Functional design patterns, Part 3, http://www.ibm.com/developerworks/java/library/j-ft12/index.html
- Functional error handling with Either and Option,http://www.ibm.com/developerworks/java/library/j-ft13/index.html
- Either trees and pattern matching, http://www.ibm.com/developerworks/java/library/j-ft14/index.html

- Rethinking dispatch, http://www.ibm.com/developerworks/java/library/j-ft15/index.html
- Tons of transformations, http://www.ibm.com/developerworks/java/library/j-ft16/index.html
- Transformations and optimizations, http://www.ibm.com/developerworks/java/library/j-ft17/index.htm
- Laziness, Part 1, http://www.ibm.com/developerworks/java/library/j-ft18/index.html
- Laziness, Part 2, http://www.ibm.com/developerworks/java/library/j-ft19/index.html
- Why functional programming is on the rise,http://www.ibm.com/developerworks/java/library/j-ft20/index.htm

[Nataflin13-14] Maurice Nataflin, Lambda FAQ,
- http://www.lambdafaq.org

[Sutter05] Herb Sutter, The Free Lunch is Over, A Fundamental Turn Toward Concurrency in Software, 2005, Dr. Dobbs
- http://www.gotw.ca/publications/concurrency-ddj.htm

Java 8
- http://openjdk.java.net/projects/jdk8/features
- http://cr.openjdk.java.net/~briangoetz/lambda/lambda-libraries-final.html
- http://cr.openjdk.java.net/~briangoetz/lambda/lambda-state-final.html
- http://cr.openjdk.java.net/~briangoetz/lambda/sotc3.html
- http://www.slideshare.net/slideshow/embed_code/15339485
- http://openjdk.java.net/projects/jdk8/milestones
- http://docs.oracle.com/javase/8/docs/api/
- http://docs.oracle.com/javase/8/docs/api/java/util/stream/Stream.html
- http://docs.oracle.com/javase/8/docs/api/java/util/stream/IntStream.html
- http://docs.oracle.com/javase/8/docs/api/java/util/Optional.html
- http://docs.oracle.com/javase/8/docs/api/java/util/OptionalInt.html
- http://docs.oracle.com/javase/8/docs/api/java/util/function/Function.html
- http://docs.oracle.com/javase/8/docs/api/java/util/function/Predicate.html
- http://docs.oracle.com/javase/8/docs/api/java/util/function/Consumer.html
- http://docs.oracle.com/javase/8/docs/api/java/util/function/Supplier.html
- http://docs.oracle.com/javase/8/docs/api/java/util/Collection.html
- http://docs.oracle.com/javase/8/docs/api/java/util/Map.html
- http://docs.oracle.com/javase/8/docs/api/java/util/List.html
- http://docs.oracle.com/javase/8/docs/api/java/util/Set.html
- http://docs.oracle.com/javase/8/docs/api/java/util/Iterator.html

- http://docs.oracle.com/javase/8/docs/api/java/lang/Iterable.html
- http://docs.oracle.com/javase/8/docs/api/java/util/Comparator.html
- http://docs.oracle.com/javase/8/docs/api/java/util/Spliterator.html
- http://docs.oracle.com/javase/8/docs/api/java/util/logging/Logger.html
- http://www.lambdafaq.org/what-are-the-reasons-for-the-restriction-to-effective-immutability/
- https://blogs.oracle.com/javaone/entry/the_javaone_2013_technical_keynote
- http://medianetwork.oracle.com/video/player/2685720528001

The BGGA project
- http://www.javac.info/

Tail-call optimization
- http://mail.openjdk.java.net/pipermail/mlvm-dev/2010-October/002017.html
- http://www.ssw.uni-linz.ac.at/Research/Papers/Schwaighofer09Master/schwaighofer09master.pdf
- https://blogs.oracle.com/jrose/entry/tail_calls_in_the_vm

Trampolining
- http://en.wikipedia.org/wiki/Tail_call

Quicksort
- http://en.wikipedia.org/wiki/Quicksort

Invoke dynamic
- https://wikis.oracle.com/display/HotSpotInternals/Method+handles+and+invokedynamic
- http://wiki.jvmlangsummit.com/Lambda_Forms:_IR_for_Method_Handles

Object oriented programming
- http://en.wikipedia.org/wiki/Object-oriented_programming

Imperative programming
- http://en.wikipedia.org/wiki/Imperative_programming

Declarative programming
- http://en.wikipedia.org/wiki/Declarative_programming

Logic programming
- http://en.wikipedia.org/wiki/Logic_programming

Fluent interface
- http://en.wikipedia.org/wiki/Fluent_interface

Design patterns
- http://www.cs.uni.edu/~wallingf/patterns/papers/fdpe2002/fdpe2002-presentation.pdf
- http://www.infoq.com/presentations/Functional-Design-Patterns
- http://www.cs.uni.edu/~wallingf/patterns/

Functional programming
- http://blog.enfranchisedmind.com/2009/07/what-is-a-functional-programming-language
- http://en.wikipedia.org/wiki/Functional_programming

Currying
- http://en.wikipedia.org/wiki/Currying
- http://www.crockford.com/javascript/www_svendtofte_com/code/curried_javascript/index.html

Higher order functions
- http://en.wikipedia.org/wiki/Higher-order_function
- http://learnyouahaskell.com/higher-order-functions
- http://en.wikibooks.org/wiki/F_Sharp_Programming/Higher_Order_Functions

Monads
- http://en.wikipedia.org/wiki/Monad_%28functional_programming%29
- http://www.haskell.org/haskellwiki/Monad
- http://c2.com/cgi/wiki?OnMonads

Referential transparency
- http://en.wikipedia.org/wiki/Referential_transparency_%28computer_science%29
- http://c2.com/cgi/wiki?ReferentialTransparency

Groovy
- http://en.wikipedia.org/wiki/Groovy_(programming_language))

JVM languages
- http://en.wikipedia.org/wiki/JVM_languages

Lambda calculus
- http://en.wikipedia.org/wiki/Lambda_calculus

Alonzo Chruch

- http://en.wikipedia.org/wiki/Alonzo_Church

LISP

- http://en.wikipedia.org/wiki/Lisp_(programming_language))

ILISP

- http://en.wikipedia.org/wiki/ISLISP

Common LISP

- http://en.wikipedia.org/wiki/Common_Lisp

OCaml

- http://en.wikipedia.org/wiki/OCaml

ML

- http://en.wikipedia.org/wiki/ML_(programming_language))

Clojure

- http://en.wikipedia.org/wiki/Clojure

Scheme

- http://en.wikipedia.org/wiki/Scheme_(programming_language))

Erlang

- http://en.wikipedia.org/wiki/Erlang_(programming_language))

Haskell

- http://en.wikipedia.org/wiki/Haskell_(programming_language))

Simula

- http://en.wikipedia.org/wiki/Simula_programming_language

Smalltalk

- http://en.wikipedia.org/wiki/Smalltalk_(programming_language))

Eiffel

- http://en.wikipedia.org/wiki/Eiffel_(programming_language))

Algol

- http://en.wikipedia.org/wiki/ALGOL

Closures in Java
- http://www.youtube.com/watch?v=yUmWQHzN5ZU&feature=gv

Scala vs. Java
- http://www.infoq.com/articles/java-8-vs-scala

Moore's Law
- http://en.wikipedia.org/wiki/Moore%27s_law

Perfect numbers
- http://en.wikipedia.org/wiki/List_of_perfect_numbers

Prime numbers
- http://en.wikipedia.org/wiki/Prime_number

Big O notation
- http://en.wikipedia.org/wiki/Big_o_notation

Windows timeline
- http://en.wikipedia.org/wiki/Timeline_of_Microsoft_Windows

Intel timeline
- http://en.wikipedia.org/wiki/List_of_Intel_microprocessors

Events of 1996
- http://www.infoplease.com/year/1996.html

The 3 stooges
- http://en.wikipedia.org/wiki/The_Three_Stooges

www.ingramcontent.com/pod-product-compliance
Lightning Source LLC
Chambersburg PA
CBHW080409060326
40689CB00019B/4187